A CHURCH WITHOUT WALLS

A CHURCH WITHOUT WALLS

By

Jean Koberlein

© Copyright 1990 — Jean Koberlein

All rights reserved. This book is protected under the copyright laws of the United States of America. This book may not be copied or reprinted for commercial gain or profit. The use of short quotations or occasional page copying for personal or group study is permitted and encouraged. Permission will be granted upon request. Unless otherwise identified, Scripture quotations are from The Revised Standard Version of the Bible.

Destiny Image Publishers
P.O. Box 351
Shippensburg, PA 17257

"Speaking to the Purposes of God for this Generation"

ISBN 1-56043-054-0

For Worldwide Distribution
Printed in the U.S.A.

THANKSGIVING AND PRAISE TO THE FATHER

For my sisters in Christ who have allowed me to share their testimonies and prayers with the Body of Christ.

>Catherine (Cappy)
>
>Charlotte
>
>Cindy
>
>Diane
>
>Linda
>
>Jacqueline (Jackie)

For Lorie and her many hours of editing and prayer.

For my husband, Ivan, for his encouragement to "Be who you are, Jean," and his constant reminder to "always keep one foot on the ground." His freedom in Christ allows me to "fly with the eagles," and his solid foundation in the Word of God reminds me to stand firmly on the Rock.

This book is dedicated to the pastors
of Charismatic Renewal
and their wives
and to those who have loved them and prayed
for them without ceasing.

Table of Contents

Introduction 1
A Church Without Walls 5
A Letter of Testimony to Those
Who Desire to Hear the Voice of Jesus 15
  "Be not afraid to listen to My voice."
A Letter of Caution to the
Watchmen Upon the Walls 49
  "Be not afraid to hear the battle cry for holiness!"
A Letter of Inner Healing to Those
who Hear the Shepherd's Call 73
  "Be not afraid to walk in the valley with Me."
A Letter of Faith to Those Who
Desire to See Miracles in Their Lives 91
  "Be not afraid to reach for a miracle!"
A Letter of Encouragement to Those
Who Will Pass Through Spiritual Seasons 113
  "Be not afraid to grow in My vineyard."
A Letter of Decision to Those
Who Are Called to Choose 127
  "Be not afraid of new wineskins."
A Letter of Confirmation to Those
Who Experience the Miracle of Birth 147
  "Be not afraid of the rebirth of My Church."
A Letter of Anticipation to Those
Who Wait for the Bridegrooms's Return 157
  "Be not afraid to prepare for My return."
A Letter of Instruction to
a Church Without Walls 171

Introduction

This book is about walls — walls within us and around us. Some of these walls offer a false sense of security or a place to hide. Others lock us into a certain mindset and religious experience. Walls have two sides and walls always divide.

My husband and I joined many of you on the road of Charismatic Renewal with a vision of Church unity in our hearts and the Word of God on our lips. What happened? We cried out against the walls of tradition and religiousity, but ended up building higher walls of fear and misunderstanding.

For years we sang praise choruses and quoted Scripture verses. We prophesied. We saw visions and dreamed dreams. Some of us even spoke in tongues, but the walls of division continued to rise.

Some built churches and then bigger churches. The

Charismatic Renewal both blessed and wounded traditional mainline denominations. But how far have we really come? And how much do we actually understand about where we've been?

This is the story of my search for understanding. Perhaps it is yours as well. For myself, and for many others in the Body of Christ, it's time for honesty. It's time to be real, to be who we are in Christ and to allow our brothers and sisters this freedom as well.

Above all, it's time to listen. The voice of Jesus is speaking to these walls built by our vain imaginations and fears and He is commanding them to come down! His Church has no such walls!

What about you? Are you ready for the walls of division in your life and ministry to come down?

Are you tired of trying to climb over, tunnel under, or make a crack in these walls in order to be the Christian you know God wants you to be or to have the ministry He wants you to have?

Are you tired of separations and divisions in the Body of Christ? Are you weary from trying to communicate with others through thick barriers of religious language and experience? Are your shoes worn out from the miles you've traveled to find the "perfect church," the one you know is out there?

If so, this book is for you!

A new wave of the Holy Spirit is coming in and the walls are coming down!

The walls of disappointment and discouragement are coming down!

The walls of pride are coming down!

The walls of fear are coming down!

The walls of misunderstanding are coming down!
The walls of tradition are coming down!
The walls of religious empires are coming down!
The walls of unforgiveness are coming down!
Listen! In the stillness of His presence, He whispers, *"Be not afraid! I'm building a Church without walls!"*

A Church Without Walls

We waited. We prayed. We trusted Jesus to open the right door.

My husband's trial sermon completed, the congregational vote taken, the President of the Church Council invited us back into the sanctuary. His words opened the door and marked the beginning of our ministry: "Reverend Koberlein, we extend to you the call to be our pastor."

We arrived with a vision and a commitment to our Lord Jesus Christ — to give the love of Jesus and to share the power of His Holy Spirit with this congregation. We wanted others to know and experience the Living God!

Moving into the large, comfortable parsonage, our three children quickly laid claim to their individual bedrooms. They cheered with delight at the prospect of living in a "real house" after four years of seminary apartments.

My husband and I looked again and again at the large brick church across the street, still finding our circumstances difficult to believe.

"Are you scared?" I asked Ivan.

"Who? Me?" He asked with a nervous laugh. Then, wrapping his arm around my waist and giving me a squeeze, he added more seriously, "I wonder what they expect of me ... and what God expects of me...."

"Oh, you're going to be a wonderful pastor," I teased him. "And of course I'll be the perfect pastor's wife!"

I allowed my thoughts to drift into the future. I saw the congregation coming alive with excitement and joy. People were expressing love for one another, reaching out in the Name of Jesus, receiving healing, and glorifying His Name.

The promises of Charismatic Renewal rang steadily in our hearts. We stood ready to lay down our lives for the sake of charismatic evangelism within our denomination. The drumbeat of evangelical leaders called us to fight against the forces of wickedness and sing a song of victory to our King!

Eight years later, almost to the day of our arrival, we stood in the yard of the parsonage once more — this time to say good-bye. Furniture and boxes filled the moving van, but disappointment and unrealized visions filled our hearts.

We'd sung the song, fought the battle, given praise to Jesus, and even laid down our lives. What had happened? What went wrong? Had we failed our God so miserably?

Ivan and I said good-bye in different ways, but we

both needed to reach for the inner resources of Christ within us. Ivan stood tall, announcing firmly, "It's over and we have a full life ahead of us ... and we're going to live it!"

Immediately he set his face and our moving van to southwest Florida. He wanted to begin again and not look back — with the warm sun on his face and the tropical sands under his feet.

I, on the other hand, needed to mourn. My mother's heart wept for the spiritual children we left behind, for the unborn spiritual babes and for those who refused to accept a new life in Christ Jesus.

Wounded and disillusioned, I wrestled with my God who had promised me so much, and, it seemed, had given so little. Nearly fourteen years of promises, dreams, visions, and prophecies since my Baptism in the Holy Spirit had all promised a fruitful ministry ... for what? To sit under a palm tree or beside a swimming pool?

"No! No!" I screamed silently at God. After the anger subsided, my heart continued to ache with an unanswered question: "Why?" And this question remained the essence of my prayers for weeks and months to follow.

But slowly the familiar voice of Jesus penetrated my wounded spirit. "It's in the songs, My daughter. The answers you seek are in the songs."

"The songs!" I cried back. "The songs didn't work! You gave them to us and promised us a Spirit-filled church. You promised us a church filled with love and miracles!"

Every time I remembered the prophetic songs given

to our small prayer community, I wept tears of disappointment and grief. We had believed their words with such faith. We had sung them together with conviction and stirred others to faith with God's prophetic promises.

For what? To have our ministry torn from us by lies and false accusations? To be physically cast aside by those we loved and trusted?

"What's happening, Lord?" I wept in confusion. "What's happening?"

Ivan watched my grief. "Let it go, Jean ... let it go," he gently encouraged me. "The past is over and we can't change what's happened. Let's be thankful for everything we have here ... in this beautiful land."

"I can't. Everything inside me aches. So much of my life has died a senseless, cruel death. I don't belong here ... I don't belong back there in the church." I buried my head in his shoulder and sobbed, "I just don't know where I belong anymore...."

I refused to let go. I needed to know — I needed to understand. Without this understanding, my entire testimony of faith in the power of my Lord stood in question.

On my knees, I continued to hear the gentle whisper, "It's in the songs."

I pulled out my guitar and tried to play. The words on the paper in front of me stared back with cold betrayal. I forced my fingers to move from chord to chord. My inner struggle stood like iron gates, locked against every note of joy.

I thought about my sisters in Christ who once sang these songs with me. I longed for our sweet fellowship together ... but it would never be the same again. A gentle breeze from the swimming pool blew the song sheets to the floor. I watched the papers scatter and felt no urge to retrieve them. My fingers loosened from the guitar strings in submission to the emotion within. "Why, Jesus? Why?"

Several years have passed since that day. Years of rest and restoration. Years of pilgrimage and prayer. Years of letting go and letting God.

The Body of Christ has been experiencing a sifting; a separation. Some call it judgment. Others call it war.

There are separations and divisions, questions and struggles. Loyalties to family, traditional religious practices, and even to God Himself are put to the test.

Christians are broken and wounded from the battle. Church buildings are no longer sanctuaries from the battle. They're too often the battleground itself.

It is imperative for us to see and understand the work taking place both within us and with us. *We are living stones, and the Father is building His Church — a Church without walls.* It is unlike any church we've known before and will be rejected by many professing Christians who continue to cling to the traditions of the past.

Jesus Christ is singing a song! Listen! His voice is ringing through the hearts of His people at this very hour, calling us to a new understanding of ministry and of what it means to be *His Church, a Church without walls.*

My people are broken, fragmented, and torn.
Just like the world on the day I was born.
Man against man, and nations at war.

Where are the people to open the door?

In churches with steeples decorated in gold.
Upstanding people, but their love has grown cold.
Words filled with jealousy, pride, and debate.
These are the people who stand in the gate?

A new Church I'm building, a house without walls.
Rooms filled with love and open to all.
A place for the weary, the broken and worn.
A place for My people to be reborn.

Living stones I am using, tried in the fire.
Raising My temple holy and high.
All for My glory, this work shall be done.
Open the door and give praise to the Son!

A Church without walls?
Is it only a vision, possible only in heavenly places?
For some, yes. And these Christians will continue to hide in fear behind their walls of tradition and historical mandates for the practice of their faith.

There are others, those with a willingness to lay down their fears; this Church will rise in splendor among them — in living rooms, in kitchens, in sanctuaries, in meeting halls, in the fields white unto harvest. The Father is building a Church without walls to give praise to His Son.

How shall we recognize this Church? She'll be known to all by her *listening heart* and her *walk of obedience*. We'll find this living temple in small fellowships of twos and threes as well as in great congregations ... in the valleys ... on the mountaintops ... and in the vineyards.

But, wherever she's found, the Bride of Christ *waits* to hear the voice of the Bridegroom and prepares herself for His soon return.

God's people are sometimes filled with fearful apprehension. Where shall we go from here? This is a way we have not traveled before and we are much afraid.

We can't go back. We can't change the past. Many of us don't belong in the places in which we find ourselves. The music in our lives is only a memory of former blessing.

In the stillness of His presence the Holy Spirit whispers to my heart and to yours, *"Be not afraid. Fear not, for the Lord your God is with you.*

"Have I not commanded you? Be strong and of good courage; be not frightened, neither be dismayed; for the Lord your God is with you wherever you go" (Joshua 1:9).

"But Jesus, there's too much fear, too many walls of tradition and security," I remind the Lord.

"Yes, My daughter, I know. I need a gentle voice to tell them ... 'Be not afraid.' "

"But *how*, Lord?"

"Write letters to My people."

"Letters?" I ask in bewilderment.

"Yes, letters."

"But what shall I say?"

"Tell My people not to be afraid of the work I am doing in this hour.... To wait in My presence and listen to My voice.... To sound the battle cry.... To grow in the vineyard.... To reach for miracles ... and to prepare for My coming. Tell them that I'm building a house without walls to give praise to the Son!"

"Who shall I send these letters to, Lord?"

"To all who will listen, to those who have ears to hear."

Thus, the Holy Spirit penned living letters on the parchment of our lives.

"He who has an ear, let him hear what the Spirit says to the churches" (Rev. 2:7, 11, 17, 29; 3:6, 13, 22).

THOUGHTS TO REMEMBER AS YOU CONTINUE TO READ

As you read the following letters (or chapters) prayerfully, one at a time, please remember that they represent focal points of growth and understanding over a period of ten years, not a testimony which takes you from beginning to end.

A congregation is a family of many members. I'm only taking you into the lives of a small number, chosen by the Holy Spirit because they and the lessons we learned together represent what has been taking place in the Body of Christ again and again.

Please don't be discouraged if only certain letters touch you at this time. Lay the others aside for a season. This little book will speak to you in many ways and at various times in your life for years to come.

Consider keeping a prayer diary as you read. Write

down your questions and thoughts for prayerful consideration. I think you'll find it interesting to see how your understanding changes and develops over the period of a few weeks or months.

It's very important for you to remember that my references to the voice of God are the *end result* of Scripture study, the still small voice of Jesus, godly counsel, personal experience, prayerful contemplation, and the test of time! *Listening prayer involves my total life in God.* Telling others what I've heard involves the use of language.

I'm praying for you as you read. May Jesus walk with you and speak to you about the "living letter" He is writing in your life today (2 Cor. 3:2-3). Amen.

Chapter One

A Letter of Testimony to Those Who Desire to Hear the Voice of Jesus

"Be not afraid to listen to My voice."

The stillness of the Holy Spirit subdued my prayers. With no more need for words or even whispers of praise, I waited silently in the presence of Jesus.

My heart filled with joy as the moments passed. The silence gave birth to an undeniable sense of God's awesome presence and the floor I sat upon became "holy ground."

Awed and humbled, I waited motionless. My body, my mind, and my spirit all felt at one with the loving presence of the Holy Spirit.

Time stood still.

Waves of Divine love welled up within me and spilled from my eyes in tears of adoration. There, in the sacred stillness, His gentle voice broke into the

A Letter of Testimony

silence and a conversation with Jesus Christ ensued deep inside my spirit.

"Teach My people to pray; teach them to enter into My presence and to listen to My voice. My heart weeps for those who do not know how to wait before Me."

My tears changed from a reflection of joy to sadness. The heart of Jesus touched mine and I wept with Him. He longed for His Church to come to Him, to be with Him, to experience His love. He waited ... *but so many just didn't know how to come.*

For a brief moment, a veil lifted from my understanding. Years of judgment against those who rejected evangelical teachings faded away. They simply *did not know how* to enter into an experience of faith with the Living God.

"Jean, teach My people to pray."

"But Lord, I've been trying to."

"No, you've been telling them *about* Me. You've been telling them *about* prayer. I want you to show them *how to listen to Me.* Prayer is communion *with Me.*"

"But, Lord..."

"You've been trying to convince them to embrace religious principles. It won't work. When they enter into My presence, I will do the work which needs to be done in their lives."

"Ask Ivan. He's the one they will listen to."

"I'm asking you, Jean."

"But Lord, he's the pastor."

"I'm asking you."

"I don't know how, Lord."

"I'll show you how ... as you listen to Me."

In spite of the Lord's call to obedience, I remained convinced. My husband should be the one to follow this word!

That very night I took advantage of a long television commercial to mention casually, "Honey, I think the Lord wants us to start a prayer group where people can learn to listen."

"To what?"

"To listen to the voice of God."

Ivan turned to me with a suspicious look. "And exactly *how* do you propose to do that?"

"I'm not sure, but..."

"Well, I certainly don't know and *please* stop coming up with projects for me. I've got enough to do!" Our conversation ended as he reached for the newspaper and opened it with a heavy sigh.

I knew my husband well enough to know his words weren't intentionally cruel, only a by-product of his continual exasperation with the level of spiritual commitment within the congregation.

I knew his struggles in ministry. The last Bible study on prayer had resulted in failure when he encouraged the women to pray out loud. *The walls of resistance stood high.* Change didn't come easily, if at all.

Our call to minister the life-changing power of Jesus Christ in the power of the Holy Spirit didn't always meet with approval. The people loved us, but it continued to remain a question of who should impress change on whom.

By the time we turned off the late night news and

started to close up the house for the night, Ivan's attitude had softened a bit.

With his arm around my shoulder he encouraged me. "Jean, be who you are. If you really believe the Lord's calling you to do something, then give it your best."

"Do you want me to forget it?" I asked with a degree of hesitancy. I didn't actually want him to say "yes," but I knew I'd have to be willing to accept his decision.

"Do you believe this idea about listening prayer is from the Lord?" he challenged me with his "pastor face."

"Yes, only I'm not certain what He wants me to do."

"If you believe it's God, then go ahead. But take it slowly and be sensitive to where the people are. Most of them aren't going to understand what you're driving at."

His warning sent a flash of doubt through my heart. Teach them to listen? Teach the members of our congregation a form of contemplative prayer practically abandoned by the modern day Church? Did anyone want to learn? And if they did, *how could I possibly teach anyone?*

I certainly didn't consider myself an expert listener by any stretch of the imagination. I struggled continually with the will and purposes of Jesus, just like all Christians.

The prophetic words which penetrated my listening ear often sent me into seasons of spiritual travail as I labored to give birth to the *understanding* of those words.

Constantly I needed to test the spirit and sometimes

I needed to lay aside a "word" because it failed to meet the test. More often than not, my husband's approving eye was the first test these words failed to meet!

Me? Teach others to listen? Yet the call from Jesus refused to leave. It rang with conviction and authority. I didn't doubt its source. I did, however, doubt my ability to follow in obedience and I continued to wrestle with it.

"Lord, how can I possibly do this thing You ask of me?"

"I am the Lord your God, who teaches you to profit, who leads you in the way you should go" (Is. 48:17).

Regardless of which way the Lord asked me to go, I knew one thing ... the danger of taking a spiritual journey alone. Spirits of deception lie on every side with treacherous plots to lead us astray. Even Jesus sent the disciples out two by two with warnings about the dangers (spiritual as well as physical) on their journeys.

My husband is and always has been my closest and dearest friend. Yet as spiritual pilgrims, we often see matters from different perspectives. Ivan keeps his feet firmly on the ground and isn't easily moved by supernatural manifestations. Each one is *thoroughly* scrutinized through a process of mental reasoning and very practical discernment. He's a teacher and all experiences of learning must submit to careful observation — especially supernatural ones! He walks with Jesus and learns "on the way" as the disciples did.

On the other hand, I'm quite happy to sit at the feet of Jesus and absorb the fulness of His presence.

Biblically-based manifestations of the Holy Spirit have taught me so much about my Lord Jesus Christ and filled me with an unquenchable desire to learn as much as I possibly can from the Scriptures and the gifts of the Holy Spirit.

Together, Ivan and I maintain a healthy balance in our walk with God and a respect for our own unique individuality in the Spirit. I love him dearly, and he me, but there are those times when I need to touch someone else who is willing to walk a path of discovery with me. This was one of those times, and God gave me Cappy.

CATHERINE (CAPPY)

Very early in our ministry, our daughter Annette bounded through the kitchen door after a short visit with Cappy. Catherine, known to all of us as "Cappy," was a young woman in her early twenties and a member of our congregation. She lived only four houses down the street.

Annette made her usual stop at the refrigerator and frowned at the slim fare. "Mom, I told Cappy about your book. She wants to read it. When are you going to go grocery shopping?"

You did what?" I asked Annette, trying to hide my surprise.

"I told you, she wants to read your book. Can I have this pizza?"

Normally, the fact that supper time was quickly approaching would have called for a quick "no." But my daughter's comment threw me off guard. She took off with the piece of pizza and I stared out the window.

At this point, *A Spiritual Encounter with the Holy One* still lay in manuscript form, typed pages bound in red notebooks. Ivan and I shared it cautiously. Our testimony exploded with strong occult and charismatic experiences. Exactly how God wanted to use it in our ministry, we simply did not know.

However, the next day I carried the heavy red notebook to Cappy. In spite of wanting to share the story with her and with anyone who wanted to read it, a strong fear swept over me. What if she didn't understand?

Cappy met me in her yard with one of her many day care children on each side. I handed her the notebook. "Annette said you wanted to read this?"

"Oh yes, why, I didn't know you had written a book." She ran her hand appreciatively over the binder and flipped through a few pages. "This really looks interesting ... are you going to have it published?"

"I'm not certain; maybe someday — if and when God opens the door."

I felt like a mother relinquishing her child into the care of a new sitter as I watched her hold my manuscript. With an unconscious movement of protectiveness, I stepped closer and added, "Right now we just share it quietly with those who express an interest."

"I gotta go potty," came a cry from the doorway, and our conversation ended.

"I'll call you when I'm finished," Cappy promised on her way across the lawn. Apprehensively, I watched Cappy and my manuscript disappear into the small yellow house.

Within a few days I sat at her kitchen table answering one question after another. My answers triggered her own story of faith as she confessed to feeling drawn to God a little more than usual lately.

After nearly an hour had passed, a silence settled in and neither one of us spoke. Finally, she took a deep breath and asked, "What is praying in tongues?"

I explained my prayer language very simply and its benefit in my own prayer life. We laughed over some lighthearted moments such as the time Annette told me, "You sound like drums, Mommy."

"You know," she said hesitantly, "I remember talking to God in a strange language when I was a little girl. Reading your book, I kept remembering those times. Do you think it's possible...?"

"Age makes no difference to the Lord." I placed my tea cup back on the table and touched her arm with a gesture of reassurance. "Certainly you might have prayed in tongues as a child. What a wonderful testimony of simple child-like faith!"

Cappy recommitted her life to Jesus. Within the next few days she asked to be baptized in the Holy Spirit, and prayed in tongues — the very language she spoke as a child.

A deep spiritual friendship started to take root. A part of my life, previously filled only with memories of dear prayer companions in other parts of the country, now exploded with new possibilities.

Cappy and I prayed together often. During our prayer times we entered the presence of Jesus together and sat quietly surrounded by His love. As a result of spending time in His presence, we experienced prayer visions and Scripture revelations. We praised together in tongues and sang freely in the spirit.

I shared the call of God now stirring inside of me with Cappy. "I know it's God, but I don't know where to begin."

Over the next few days we asked for wisdom and guidance. Having asked, we listened with open hearts to revelations such as these:

> *My people must listen. They must listen to My voice, for the trumpets and the shouts are to be heard with the hearing not given to the world. Many of My people are blind and deaf. They walk about with blinders and ear muffs. They walk about with all manner of spiritual diseases which afflict their spiritual eyes and ears. Woe to those who are not able to hear My call. Woe to those who refuse to hear My call. For My call goes forth in this hour to prepare for My coming. How many are listening? How many are listening? Woe to those who do not hear My call to preparation.*
>
> *"You are my witnesses! Bring forth the people who are blind, yet have eyes, who are deaf, yet have ears!"* (Is. 43:8)

The Lord also gave us a vision of a beautiful green oasis that grew in the midst of a desert. Green vegetation and tall palm trees grew in this place. Thirsty people came dragging in from the desert. This word followed: *"Will you be My oasis, children? I will make springs in the desert. I will revitalize My people. Come with Me. Follow Me."*

Was it truly God who spoke to us in those quiet moments we shared together — in a still small voice deep within us? We believe He did. We wrote everything down and researched supporting Scripture verses. We tested the peaceful reassurance in our hearts and submitted ourselves and our revelations to our husbands.

We sensed the *urgency* and the absolute *necessity* for Christians to enter the presence of Jesus with a surrendered heart. The time is short and the second coming of our Lord closer than ever.

And my companion in this walk? Cappy stood by my side with a committed heart and an adventurous spirit. The prospect of taking one step at a time, led by the Holy Spirit, excited us both.

United in spirit and purpose, Cappy and I took a shaking step of obedience and extended a very simple invitation to the women of our adult discussion class.

"Regardless of where you're at right now, would you like to take *one more step* of faith in your devotional life?"

Quite honestly, we expected one or two people to respond. Stunned, on that first Sunday morning, I held the names of eighteen women in my hand. Eighteen, from an average Sunday morning attendance of about 125, was not bad! In fact, it was very good.

Many sessions of prayer preceded our prayer group meetings. We prayed about every detail of this new ministry, relying totally on the wisdom of our God.

Jesus told us to share only from our personal prayer life and spiritual development ... to give a testimony of our own prayer life. A word of obedience from the Holy Spirit stirred a strong conviction within us: *"Do not lead someone else on a path that you have not first walked."*

As we prayed, Jesus filled our hearts with a new understanding and empathy for this group of women. He instructed us not to lay our personal expectations, nor the expectations of Charismatic Renewal, on anyone.

Prayers to receive Jesus as Savior, to be filled with the Holy Spirit, to be healed, etc., were to be given only as each one indicated a readiness in her heart for such ministry. The heartbeat of our ministry needed to synchronize with the heartbeat of each woman as she stepped forward in faith.

Thus, like packing away personal treasures no longer needed, I gently laid aside a vast storehouse of charismatic jargon and programmed steps to spirituality. Although these religious principles once ministered to me, I couldn't impose them upon others. Jesus knew the need in each woman's spirit and He stood ready to minister as they entered His presence.

The hour is coming, You call me to follow,
To follow Your voice within.
Your Spirit's inside me, calling me softly
And praising my Father above.
Rise up in my heart, Holy Spirit
Let me hear the voice of my Lord.

CHARLOTTE

Cappy and I held our breath and prayed silently as Charlotte walked into Cappy's kitchen the first night of our prayer group. Charlotte's strong, confident personality vibrated with every brisk step. Her glasses, hanging from a chain around her neck, sent a message

A Letter of Testimony 27

to us that she'd come to look this whole thing over very closely.

She was a new grandmother, an employee in the local Junior High School cafeteria, and a woman who knew her Bible very well — that's all I really knew about Charlotte. She had entered my adult Sunday School discussion class nearly a year before, but she spoke very little about the bundle of life wrapped up inside her. Controlled, strong, and determined — this described Charlotte. Apprehensive, weak, and trembling — this described Cappy and me that first night!

After everyone arrived we opened with a simple prayer and one question. "Why have you come? Tell us about your expectations for the next six weeks."

At Charlotte's turn she tapped her pencil on the table and took a deep breath. "I'm not sure why I'm here, but I know it's time to take a look at a few things."

Then, looking me straight in the eye, she said, "I want to know about this 'tongues' thing. I don't think it's for me, but I've got to straighten it out in my own mind."

Silence fell over our little group. Cappy and I looked at each other. The very thing we feared most had come upon us! The most controversial issue of all, the one that turned people off, split churches, and sent our denominational office into a tizzy! Tongues!

Certainly we planned to talk about tongues, but not on the first night! Charlotte sensed our uneasiness and quickly apologized for even mentioning it.

"Oh no, that's quite all right." I assured her. "We will talk about tongues and all the spiritual gifts, but you need to wait until the fourth week and then we'll answer your questions — or at least we'll try. We want to present everything in the sequence that we believe God has asked us to."

Cappy nodded in agreement as she shot me a "well done" look. I took a deep breath as Charlotte's body relaxed in her chair. Evidently, Charlotte was relieved too!

"That's fine," Charlotte replied, laying one hand on the table firmly. "I can wait."

Then Cappy shared her personal testimony. In fear and trembling, she related her story of a progressive walk with Jesus since childhood, attending church, entering Confirmation, and considering herself a Christian.

All of this rang with familiar notes to those listening. The women responded with reassuring smiles. Cappy's soft voice strengthened as she picked up confidence and moved on.

"I reached a point a little over a year ago," she told us, "when I knew I had to get serious with God. I needed to make a definite commitment and allow Jesus to be Lord of my life."

She described her recent experience of receiving the Baptism of the Holy Spirit and her prayer language. She saw it not as "something new," but as returning to the faith she had known as a child.

After Cappy's testimony we moved into a discussion about knowing Jesus as Savior and Lord. We talked frankly about coming before Him in prayer to speak words of love to Him instead of merely presenting our endless list of requests.

A Letter of Testimony 29

"Spend time this week just simply telling Jesus how much you love Him and how much He means to you. Develop your love relationship with Jesus," Cappy encouraged everyone.

"Wait in His presence and learn to recognize the peaceful stillness of the Holy Spirit. Be still before Him, still enough to hear the sound of rain drops or breezes blowing," I suggested.

"Listen for His voice in the silence ... for revelation to break through your own thoughts ... for the gentle tugs upon your heart. Expect the Holy Spirit to bring portions of Scripture to your remembrance, or words of faith spoken by a friend. Give Him time. Give Him room. Give Him space to fill with Holy revelation."

"I never used to hear Jesus say anything to me," Cappy confessed. "But then I never stopped to listen or gave Him time to speak."

The women around Cappy's table nodded in agreement. Charlotte wrote everything down very carefully.

These subjects could have filled hours, but in a short time we shared only what Jesus wanted us to share — the truth in our own prayer lives.

I tried not to notice Charlotte stiffening again in the chair beside me. The words kept coming out of my mouth as I talked about sitting silently before Jesus, but I could almost hear her loud thoughts beaming out at me: "This woman thinks she's going to change the way I pray. Why, I've been praying in my own way longer than she's been out of diapers."

I finished explaining the necessity of being quiet. "It's because the Holy Spirit dwells deep within us. This is where we communicate with our Lord — in the *stillness* where the human spirit is able to discern the softest whisper ... it's deep inside of us." Charlotte broke in.

"This isn't going to work for me. I'm a person that always has a great deal to say to God. Being quiet is not a part of my nature and He knows that. No, this isn't going to work for me."

"Well, at least give it a try," I encouraged her. "Just a few moments or a minute or two before your regular prayers — or even after them. See what happens."

We ended our first night in accordance with specific guidance from the still, small voice of Jesus. We walked in simple child-like faith. Jesus said, "Do it this way," and we did.

Laying hands upon each woman, one at a time, we prayed for the release of prayer and for the opening of spiritual eyes and ears. As we moved around the kitchen table and prayed for each one, the silence in the room intensified. Not an uncomfortable silence, but a gentle, loving stillness which welcomed the presence of the Holy Spirit.

We finished, but no one moved or spoke. One wiped a few tears. Softly, Cappy and I praised Jesus for His gentle, loving presence in our midst and reminded Him of His promise to take these women tenderly by the hand for a walk into the depths of His love.

The following week we didn't expect to see Charlotte back. Yet she arrived on time and with an open spirit.

"This isn't easy for me," she reminded us. "I wasn't going to come. I've prayed in my own way for a long time."

When we asked for reactions to the experiment of

keeping a spiritual diary for the past week, however, Charlotte spoke up first. "Oh, I wrote pages and pages." She rubbed her hand appreciatively over her prayer diary. (We had given each one a small spiral notebook with the homework assignment of writing a letter to Jesus each day, as well as recording prayer requests, meaningful Scriptures, and what they believed Jesus might be saying to them in return.)

But in spite of this glimmer of promise, Charlotte faced a major obstacle. It had surfaced on our very first night and surprised us all. Although a well-respected Bible teacher and church leader, Charlotte was actually *afraid* of the supernatural! She envisioned any kind of spiritual experience as relinquishing control to an outside force.

We tried to assure her, "Jesus doesn't violate your will or your self-control. You'll always be in control of the Holy Spirit within you. Only satan violates people by taking over."

But her fears persisted. She listened to us with a guarded curiosity and sharp defenses, rejecting most of our prayer experiences as a possibility for her own life.

Week after week Charlotte arrived with a grocery list of questions. Her thirst for truth intensified with each week and she accepted her own responsibility in the learning process with spiritual maturity.

"I know I have a lot to learn about all of this and I don't expect you to give me all the answers. God and I are doing a great deal of talking these days."

Occasionally Charlotte trusted us enough to openly share past pain. Her spiritual walk had taken her through many difficult places. Just a few years ago, while on the very brink of evangelical zeal in her teaching ministry, denominational authorities rebuked her for proclaiming the soon coming of our Lord Jesus Christ. Since then she walked carefully, secure in God, but very insecure in the family of God.

Then, near the end of the six weeks, Charlotte approached me after our adult Sunday School class. "I have to tell you something, Jean. Something's happened to me..."

The look in her eyes asked for reassurance even before the words tumbled out of her mouth — as if I might reject her. "I saw Jesus! He spoke to me!"

"What happened?" I asked in amazement, pulling her down to the chair beside me.

"I was praying, 'Jesus, what do You want me to do for You? Show me the way. Lord Jesus, please help and protect our Healing Service.' Then I saw Him. I saw Jesus standing in front of the clouds. He was dressed in a long white robe." With dramatic gestures she described the vision. I listened, stunned, as she continued.

"He held His right hand out and toward me, as if in an appeal. In His left hand and arm was a large round basket about three inches deep. It was tipped forward, empty. And then I heard Him say loudly, '*Fill My basket*'!"

"Oh Charlotte, that's wonderful! How did you hear His voice? In your mind, or was it a deep knowing inside your spirit?"

"No, I *heard* Him."

I backed up a little bit and said more slowly, "You mean you heard a loud mental voice?"

A Letter of Testimony 33

"No Jean," she said emphatically. "I heard Him with my ears ... it was just as real as you are talking to me right now. *'Fill My basket!'* I didn't know what to do. I pulled the covers up over my head. For a few seconds I thought I'd lost my mind. My heart raced like crazy. But I know it was Jesus; I know it was."

I pulled myself together and put my Sunday School books down on the floor. Charlotte of all people! She didn't seem to notice my surprise and kept right on talking.

"I don't know what it means. I don't know what He wants me to do, but there's something that I must do for Jesus, I know that!"

She had heard Jesus speak in an audible voice! Not only did she *hear* Him, but she *saw* Him! The prayer ministry worked! Jesus was doing exactly as He had promised: *"Show them how to come into My presence and I'll do the work that needs to be done in their lives."*

I put my arms around her with a big hug. "Charlotte, you'll know exactly what He wants. Keep praying. He's faithful and will guide you every step of the way."

The next week Charlotte came back again, confessing quietly that she'd entered the ranks of "one of those people."

"Every morning my dog and I go for a walk and that's my time to talk things over with the Lord. I wear my pollen mask so I can pray and sing and there's no one to hear me but my dog and Jesus. Well, I'd been praying all these weeks, 'Lord teach me to pray.' I didn't want this tongues thing. I just wanted to learn to pray more effectively.

"One morning some words slipped out that I didn't recognize. Well, I stopped right there. But the next morning a few more slipped out! I went home and dug out my old Latin books, certain I'd just made it up myself from an old memory. But you know, I can't find those words anywhere!"

She continued, "As afraid as I was, and as much as I didn't want this gift, it is one of the most beautiful experiences I've ever had." Her voice rang with love and adoration for Jesus. "He answered my prayer, but not in the way I thought He would."

Within a few weeks Charlotte allowed Jesus to set her free from still another fear. From the very beginning she let us know in no uncertain terms that she didn't want other people to know too much about her.

"There are parts of my life that I don't want other people walking around in!" she insisted.

Charlotte's walls of privacy stood very high. But God, the "author and finisher of our faith," continued to do His work and Charlotte eventually stepped in as co-leader of the third, fourth, and fifth prayer groups, openly sharing about her prayer experiences so that others might be able to enter the presence of Jesus as she had learned to.

God's timing is always perfect. He called Charlotte forth to minister and at the same time He released Cappy to prepare for the birth of her first child.

Cappy and I had expected so little and received so very much from our small steps of obedience. To see such change in one person's life, as we had witnessed in Charlotte's, caused us to stand in awe of our Heavenly Father's wisdom. He met her in the secret places of her heart and heard her cry.

As we did from Charlotte, and from others to follow, we continued to hear one desperate plea: *"Help me, I am afraid of God."* And, in a gentle voice to a people much afraid, we continued to say, *Be not afraid ... to listen to Him."*

DIANE

Diane, a young mother and elementary school teacher, joined our first group with Charlotte. A perfectionist in every sense of the word, Diane always walked through the door promptly at 7:30, neatly dressed and ready to give us her complete attention. She gave Cappy and me much more respect than either of us felt we deserved, always acknowledging us as leaders and teachers.

"I know I need something in my spiritual life," Diane confessed her first night. "I don't think I'm ready for all of this, but I've made a commitment to come and," taking a deep breath, "I'm going to see this through."

From the very beginning Diane laid her honest feelings on the table. "I do not accept change easily. It takes me a long time to look something over and feel comfortable with new ideas."

Every week Diane's words expressed fear.

"I'm afraid of change."

"I'm afraid that God will change me into someone that I don't want to be."

"I'm afraid this will upset my husband and my parents."

Week after week she listened quietly, asking occasional questions, but giving little response to a definite step of faith. That is, until the fifth week.

After each session we practiced a time of listening prayer together. Beginning with a time of gentle praise, we turned to Jesus — to the presence of His Holy Spirit within us and around us. In the stillness we waited, not speaking or praying aloud but just waiting for His love to touch each one of us.

During our prayer time on the fifth week, Diane broke into tears and spoke in a trembling voice, "I'm so afraid of You, God. I don't want to be, but I am. Please help me."

Gently, we joined in prayer for Diane, not wanting to disturb the quiet work of the Spirit taking place within her.

Very simply and quietly we asked Jesus to deliver Diane from her fears and to help her take the next step of faith.

Within a few moments Diane asked for the Baptism in the Holy Spirit. Her honest confession of fear and her willingness to trust Jesus stilled the fears which had haunted her.

In the months and years to come, Diane would be a strong, steady influence among us. She, like Charlotte, received the gift of prophetic vision and a renewed willingness to serve Jesus within the congregation.

The changes she so greatly feared didn't happen. Instead, Jesus enhanced the beauty already growing within her personality and spirit. He added the gift of prudence to her natural sense of cautiousness. Diane's willingness to wait for God's time would keep her and many of us from running ahead of our Lord's plans.

Oh, Jesus, thank You for setting Your people free from fear! Thank You for using such imperfect vessels as Cappy and I. Thank You for reminding us that it's Your love, not our abilities, which makes the difference for women like Diane.

CINDY

The first prayer group ended after the scheduled six weeks, and a second group formed. Cindy asked me to visit with her at home. Cappy and I encouraged the women to ask for personal ministry, realizing that many felt hesitant to share inner feelings of faith or ask for prayer in a group setting.

There, at Cindy's kitchen table, she described a deep current of fear filtering through her life — from the fear of God Himself to an intense fear of the dark.

Cindy and her husband Kerry had recently transferred to our congregation. Cindy attended our daytime mothers' discussion group.

Alive and vibrant, Cindy's enthusiasm for life spilled over into her experience of faith. Every new discovery about Jesus sent lights dancing in her eyes, reflecting child-like excitement.

A life-long Lutheran, however, Cindy rebelled at fundamental religious terms. The morning we discussed the "born-again" experience in the mothers' group, her back stiffened with resistance as she retorted, "Those people think they're something special!"

But after sharing her own experience of receiving Jesus as Savior at a Billy Graham movie she started to understand that she fell into the ranks of "those people."

Yet here, in her sunny kitchen, our conversation

uncovered a part of her life lying locked behind closed doors — *the fear of experiencing the supernatural presence of God.*

"I've learned so much about Jesus and the Holy Spirit. I want to experience all this for myself, but I'm afraid. I've tried not to be. I've prayed and it just doesn't seem to do any good. I can't help it. I go so far with my prayers and then *something* is always there — stopping me."

"Well, we'll just ask Jesus to set you free. He will," I told her confidently.

"How?"

"I'm not sure ... we'll just start praying and allow the Holy Spirit to guide our prayers. The Spirit knows how to pray so much better than we do."

Just the prospect of entering into an unknown prayer sent Cindy back in her seat a few inches. But she bit her lip and whispered, "Ooooo-k."

We started to pray. We praised Jesus for His love and I asked Him to set Cindy free from the fear which gripped her, confidently rebuking the powers of darkness. I affirmed in prayer, "In God there is no fear ... perfect love casts out fear."

Cindy squeezed my hands tightly, "Something's happening!"

"What is it?" I asked. "Just tell me what you're feeling as we pray."

"I'm spinning. The inside of my head is spinning ... faster and faster."

Quietly but firmly I bound the spirit of fear in the Name of Jesus and demanded its departure. Within a few moments Cindy remarked with a look of surprise,

"It stopped. The spinning stopped..." She asked curiously, "What was that?"

"A spirit of fear," I told her gently.

"Ohhhh. That sounds serious. I could really feel something. But it's gone now."

Early in our prayer group sessions we discussed "spiritual housecleaning" and the importance of renouncing the forces of satan. Cindy understood all of this intellectually. Now she understood it experientially.

"Satan has lots of little tricks up his sleeve to keep us away from God," I assured her. Sitting back in my chair I silently thanked Jesus for doing such a quick and gentle work in Cindy's life.

"Whew! I'm glad that's taken care of," Cindy exclaimed with a look of amazement.

She slept without the hall light on that night — the first time since childhood. The shadows of darkness no longer held her in bondage.

The following week Cappy and I praised God as we prayed with Cindy for the Baptism in the Holy Spirit. A few days later, without any prompting, Cindy witnessed to the power of her deliverance and her Spirit Baptism with a striking confidence and boldness.

Her testimony sent a message to all of us: *"Stand boldly in My Name and tell others about the work I've done in your life."*

Forgive us, Lord, and thank You for sending Cindy to remind us again that "In God there is no fear."

LINDA

The prayer ministry not only revealed fear. It uncovered hidden truth.

Beautiful faith experiences lie buried, locked away deep inside the hearts of many Believers. The presence of Jesus is rejected with fearful misgivings because such experiences are misunderstood. Thus, the Holy Spirit is pushed away in fear.

Linda's presence in the mothers' group often spoke more loudly than her words. She contributed very little to our discussion and stayed away from making long-term commitments with others. Her entire life centered in her two young daughters and husband, Ron.

Once, very quietly, Linda shared, "I over-committed myself in our old church and I've made a promise not to make that mistake again. I must have time for my family."

Linda attended our fourth Prayer Group. Although she had signed up at the very first invitation, each time a new group formed, Linda found some reason not to attend. Finally, she joined us to take one more step in her devotional life.

One evening she lingered long after everyone else left, not moving from the large green chair in the corner of Ivan's office. I sat down beside her and waited quietly. I waited ... and waited ... and waited!

The words wouldn't — or couldn't — come out of her mouth. I prayed quietly in tongues. Finally, with trembling lips and with tears spilling out of her eyes, Linda spoke.

"I had to make myself come to this. Every time you offered a group I found some good reason not to come, but this time I just couldn't find one — no matter how hard I looked.

"I have to find out what's happening to me. I had to come. I just don't understand. I've always been close to Jesus. But, Jean, I've been seeing things in my prayers and I have strange feelings about people that I know and even people that I don't know.

"You talked about the occult and how sometimes satan does these things. I love God, but I'm not sure what's going on. Sometimes I even think I'm losing my mind."

Her voice trailed off and the tears ran down her face. I placed my hand on her arm and prayed gently in tongues. The peace and love of Jesus Christ radiated from her spirit — not the satanic deception she so greatly feared or the turmoil of a disturbed mind.

The Holy Spirit within me literally danced with joy as I prayed for her. I wanted to laugh in holy delight for Linda. The simple gift of prophecy rolled up and out of my spirit with a special sense of God's pleasure.

"Linda, it's the Lord Jesus that's speaking to you. You're experiencing promptings from the Holy Spirit for intercessory prayer. He's called you to the ministry of intercession for His people. He wants you to know there's nothing abnormal about you or your prayer experiences — the *supernatural* will become *natural* to you as you allow Jesus to teach you wonderful things about Himself and the ministry He's calling you to."

The tears stopped and she listened intently, absorbing every word. "I just had to be certain. I didn't understand ... I've never learned about these things before. All the years I've been raised in the Church and no one has ever told me that it's possible to experience God like this. Why didn't they tell me? Why? Why didn't someone tell me? All these years..."

Her question wasn't just for me. Her searching thoughts confronted many of the Christians she'd known since childhood. So many Christians, so much fear, and so little understanding.

I didn't have the answers she wanted, but I did have a question for her.

"Linda, have you asked for the Baptism in the Holy Spirit?"

"No, I was afraid to. But I do want to."

"Then let's pray right now."

We prayed and the anointing of the Holy Spirit fell upon both of us with intensity. Neither one of us wanted to speak. We simply entered into a time of sacred silence before Jesus.

After a time, I opened my eyes and watched Linda sitting quietly in prayer. No longer strained and tense, her expression conveyed contentment and peace. She reached out for her Lord and He touched her.

"Oh Jesus," my heart cried, "Your Church is filled with fear. You're trying to give Yourself to us and we're so afraid. You're pouring Your gifts out upon us and we don't understand them. How long will these *walls of misunderstanding* divide us?

"Why can't we teach these things openly without condemnation — without rejection? Life-long Church members are afraid of God! Why? How many Lindas are You calling out to? How many, Lord?"

JACKIE

If someone missed a meeting for an emergency, we tried to meet with her personally. The Holy Spirit impressed upon us the importance of teaching in continuous steps, one building one upon another. Spiritual hop-scotch creates a dangerous path, often leading to deception and spiritual confusion.

Jackie lived next door. A junior high school teacher and our Christian Education chairperson, Jackie arrived at her first group meeting and stated determinedly, "I want to experience God. I've grown up in the Church. I know a great deal about Him, but I want to experience my faith."

In spite of Jackie's apparent open-mindedness, I knew our prayer ministry stood on trial the moment she walked through the door. Her suspicions about me and the prayer groups ran fairly high — about an eight on a scale of one to ten!

She was already doing some reading about prophecy and evangelical leaders who openly proclaimed that God speaks to His people today. Although curious and filled with a spiritual hunger, the idea of *hearing God speak to people* didn't fit together neatly with traditional Lutheranism.

Of all meetings, Jackie managed to miss the day we discussed the Baptism of the Holy Spirit. However, she did agree to meet with Charlotte and me after a committee meeting one night.

There, in our Church Council room, Charlotte and I shared our own testimonies with straightforward simplicity. Finishing, we waited for Jackie's questions.

"I can't say that I've ever had anything like that happen to me. I've felt really close to God at times, but I don't think I've received this 'Baptism in the Spirit' that you're talking about. I've always asked God to fill me with His Spirit, but no, I've never really experienced anything supernatural. But," she added with sincerity, "I'd like to."

I shot a quick look at Charlotte. We both relaxed. Jackie's honest quest to experience God set us free to minister to her.

Jackie continued, "This week I found a place in the Book of Acts [Chapter 19] where the people asked, 'Did you receive the Holy Spirit?' And they answered, 'We didn't even know there was a Holy Spirit.'

"I guess I feel like that. Of course I always knew the Holy Spirit existed, but not about *experiencing* Him."

"Do you want us to pray for you now?" I asked her. "Sometimes it's helpful to have others lay hands on you in prayer for the Baptism in the Holy Spirit. We agree together in prayer and join our faith with yours."

She looked up at me uneasily, "Do I *have* to pray in tongues?"

Both Charlotte and I laughed, remembering the same fears expressed by so many. "No, not unless you want to — that's completely up to you. God will not violate your free will. The gift is yours when you're ready to receive it. Take one step at a time," I encouraged her with a smile.

"Well, I think I do want that gift. But I'm not ready yet."

As Jesus instructed us, we ministered only as the women expressed a desire and a hunger in their heart. Charismatic doctrines about when one should receive the gift of tongues laid aside, we walked in obedience to our call from Jesus. "Do not lay expectations of faith

A Letter of Testimony 45

upon anyone. Give each one the freedom to follow Me step by step."

Charlotte and I laid hands on our sister in Christ and prayed softly, asking Jesus to baptize her with His Holy Spirit. After a short prayer in English we moved into tongues, allowing the Holy Spirit to offer the perfect prayer of praise and intercession for Jackie.

Jackie's body, tense as we started to pray, relaxed and rested back against the sofa. Her hand slipped from mine in complete relaxation and her facial expression indicated a restful and loving encounter with her Lord.

Charlotte and I stopped praying. We waited in silence for Jackie's response. Slowly, as if waking up from a deep sleep, she opened her eyes and stared at us with wide-eyed amazement.

"I saw something ... it was a beautiful calm ocean, a bright blue sky. I've never seen such a beautiful blue. A large white dove flew across the water. I just kept watching it fly and as the dove flew, the whitecaps on the water formed letters. They spelled out, *'I am here.'* Then the dove flew off to the horizon and a word formed in the clouds ... *'Wait.'* "

Excitedly, we talked about her vision. God had etched a prophetic call deep in her heart — to wait for Him, for His word, for His time.

She hungered for more of the God she had known since childhood. He filled her with abundant life and put a new song in her heart!

Oh, God created the world
  Yes He made it just for us
He put the sun and the moon

And the stars up above
He placed the fish in the sea
   And the leaves on the trees
Yes, He made all this for you and for me.

He placed the birds in the air
   He gave us His own Son
So that our lives may be spared
   and óre the Devil He won
Sweet Jesus died on a tree
   Now our salvation is sure
If we only believe, we'll have life evermore.

Songs of thanksgiving we owe
   To our God up above
Who will help guide our lives
   With the sign of a dove
Out of the deep blue sky
   He sent a Helper my way
Over troubled waters He came
   To turn deep night into day.

The Holy Spirit is here
   He's here for everyone
No matter who you may be
   He completes God's Trinity
God's truth He came to reveal
   If we just ask Him to stay
Then to the Father, Son, and Spirit we pray.

                                                JG*

*All songs noted JG are written by Jackie

A Letter of Testimony

The six women you have just met through these pages dared to step across the line of safe spirituality as prescribed by religious tradition. They laid down their fears and trusted in the omnipotent God of their childhoods.

They placed their hands in the hand of Jesus, their Savior and Lord.

They opened their hearts to receive the Holy Spirit, their Teacher and Guide.

These women joined the thousands of men and women around the world who are entering the presence of Jesus Christ and are receiving His prophetic word for this hour.

Everywhere they gather, their lives form a room in *God's house without walls*. They minister His love in word and deed with power and authority. They sing songs of healing in a broken world and pray expectantly for their Lord's return.

They are living stones in God's house without walls.

Suggested Scripture Meditation: First Peter 2:4-5
                                  Isaiah 66:1-2

Chapter Two

A Letter of Caution to the Watchmen upon the Walls

"Be not afraid to hear the battle cry for holiness!"

A cry is coming forth from the heavens. It calls God's people to holiness. The trumpet sounds and we rise with the weapons of warfare to meet our enemy.

The preachers preach, the teachers teach, the evangelists proclaim and the prophets speak.

Everyone calls the Body of Christ to move forward into battle and to take up the authority of Christ over the evil one.

The troops are assembled, the weapons dispersed. A battle shout echoes through the camp — "Satan, begone in the Name of Jesus!"

The demons tremble and scurry from one abode to another like frightened mice at the sound of heavy footsteps, while the Christians cheer and applaud one another for their fearless battle strategies and powerful words of warfare.

But where is the victory?

Why is the Body of Christ broken and torn?

Why do congregations divide and destroy one another?

Why are fellowships which once testified to mighty works in the Name of Jesus now only memories?

Why have denominational renewal movements retrogressed into institutional organizations which look more and more like the churches they were birthed to renew?

Why do Christians move from one fellowship to another, always searching for the home they never seem to find?

"Why, Lord?"

My husband and I asked these questions over and over again. We believed in spiritual warfare. My own spiritual birth had taken place in the midst of a violent spiritual battle.

We knew the enemy. We knew how to stand against him in the Name of Jesus. Yet all of our experiences and our knowledge about the powers of darkness did not equip us to understand the battle cry for holiness.

Therefore we found ourselves enrolled in a school led by the Holy Spirit. The requirement for graduation: repentance.

At a clergy retreat, with several other pastoral couples, God radically challenged my understanding of spiritual renewal. Ivan and I both ached with a hunger to hear from God and we continued to pray for the renewal of our congregation. Yet the answers to our prayers far exceeded our limited understanding of God's renewal plans.

During the retreat a number of hours were set aside from teaching and fellowship for personal prayer and contemplation.

After the early afternoon session our speaker dismissed us and everyone quietly separated, moving to find a place for prayerful communion with the Lord. Ivan picked up his Bible from under the chairs in front of us and told me, "I'm going to go outside for a walk."

His eyes sent me an invitation to join him and my thoughts moved in the direction of following him, but my body remained planted firmly on the chair. Within a few moments I found myself alone in the meeting room — alone with Jesus.

In the undeniable stillness of His presence, an insistent voice called to me from a depth beyond conscious thought.

"My people are playing war games."

As is so often the case when Jesus speaks, a deep inner knowing accompanied His word. In my mind's eye I saw untold numbers of Spirit-filled Christians, armed with the Word of God and dressed in the full armor of the Spirit. They moved out with shouts against the enemy, but instead of facing the evil one they turned on each other while the demons cheered with delight from the sidelines.

As I heard the prophetic word, a dramatic scene unfolded before me and I felt the unending patience of our Heavenly Father who waited for the war games to cease.

Although you and I must never totally depend upon

A Letter of Caution

our feelings, I believe there are specific moments when our awesome God speaks to us and we have nothing else but a rush of inner responses. They light up our innermost being like a dazzling display of fireworks.

Understand it? Express it? Sometimes we stand helpless.

"My people are playing war games!"

I felt a oneness with this truth. I believed it. I received it. I both ached with the heart of the Father for His people and bowed before His throne in repentance. Immersed in an emotional interaction with my God, I accepted a wisdom much higher than my own.

His prophetic word, planted in my spirit like a fertilized egg in the womb of a woman, needed time to develop within me, in due season to give birth to full understanding.

Forgive me, Lord Jesus, for aborting the precious seeds of Your prophetic word before they come to full maturity and give birth to *understanding* in my heart.

Our retreat ended as quietly as it began. Only the passing of time and the never-ending school of the Holy Spirit would help me to understand the events which had transpired within my spirit.

Back home, our Wednesday night healing ministry continued. Here in the midst of organized religion and denominational traditions, the Holy Spirit created an oasis for us to experience His love and presence in ways which refreshed our spirits and encouraged us to keep pressing on in Him.

At times, a few of us gathered for prayer before the

service. One such night Ivan, Jackie and I approached the Lord in prayer with an unusual anticipation building in our spirits.

We praised, we prayed, and we listened. The peaceful presence of God's Spirit settled in and around us. As was our custom, we openly shared the inspiration of the Holy Spirit with one another.

One of us had a vision; a picture of broken vessels by the edge of a stream. Flowing water mixed with mud and gravel formed the bank of the stream. This blended together with the broken pieces and made them whole again. They were no longer broken vessels, but *serving dishes.*

The Lord gave a word of prophecy: "This is a time of preparation, My children. Soon you will cross the rivers of the Jordan. But first, there are things in your life which must be removed."

We were also given Isaiah chapter sixteen. We turned to the Scripture passage, and midway through the chapter I cringed as the words stabbed my heart.

> We have heard of the pride of Moab,
> how proud he was;
> of his arrogance, his pride, and his insolence —
> his boasts are false.
> Therefore let Moab wail,
> let everyone wail for Moab.
>
> Isaiah 16:6-7a

The downfall of Moab — *pride.* This word continually appeared in our prayers, in visions, in Scripture, in prophecy.

What did Jesus mean?

A Letter of Caution 55

We prayed.
We confessed.
We continued to hear the Holy Spirit reprimand us.
"Why, Lord?"
We resumed reading from Isaiah.

> ...the battle shout has fallen.
> And joy and gladness are taken away
> from the fruitful field; and in the
> vineyards no songs are sung...
> Isaiah 16:9b-10

The three of us looked at each other. We'd come to prayer expecting promises for healing and miracles, for the renewal of our congregation. Certainly not this!

"Well," Ivan remarked slowly, "It's time for the service. We need to see what God wants to do."

"Whatever it is, it's going to be interesting," commented Jackie thoughtfully.

I looked at the open Bible in my lap. The words in front of me continued to blaze with prophetic fire.

The evening service moved smoothly. We praised and worshiped with freedom and love. Ivan ministered and God's people responded with faith-filled anticipation. The difficult word about pride drifted from our thoughts.

The following week a small group of prayer warriors stayed after the Wednesday night service to intercede for the congregation with fervent prayer. We praised, we prayed, and we listened for God's word.

His word came forth: *"I know your struggle, My children, and your prayers are heard; but you do not follow My Word. You do not follow My Word. I am the Way, the Truth, and the Life. Look into My teaching for your error. You profess to use My Word and stand upon it in all things that you do. Do not say that you do when your actions prove that you do not. I know your thoughts and I know your actions. I am your Father and your Creator....*"

Jackie physically shook as she finished the prophecy. With tears in her eyes she looked at us, saying, "Something is wrong here and God isn't pleased at all. I don't like whatever it is that I'm feeling right now."

We continued in prayer, and again Jackie prophesied. "*Commandments I give you, yet you do not heed them. They are in My Word. As in the days they were given, they are still true today. Time has no bearing upon me. My children, stand steadfast in My Word. Only in this way will you be able to defeat the enemy. I am your Father. You are My children. You need to learn obedience and you shall be disciplined. Do not fear, for I am with you always. I love you. My Comforter shall give you joy when you have been corrected. I leave you mercy and love. Be steadfast in My love.*"

Chastised before God, we prayed with fearful respect. "What is it, Jesus?

"What needs to be disciplined?

"What have we done?"

My own tumbling thoughts were interrupted as Charlotte spoke out. "I keep hearing Jesus say one word," her voice faltered slowly. "The word is 'pride.' "

"God opposes the proud, but gives grace to the humble" (James 4:6b).

A Letter of Caution   57

Our prayer time ended quietly. We waited for Ivan to speak, but he stood up and headed for his office without a word.

"I wonder what he thinks we should do?" Cappy asked quietly.

Shaking my head in bewilderment, I looked at the closed door. "I don't know. You ask him."

Later, at home, I challenged Ivan as if our entire relationship with God rested upon his shoulders. "Well, what *are* we going to do?"

"Do? I'm not going to do anything."

"Well, we can't just sit here after what we've heard and not do something."

"First of all, Jean, I'm not sure exactly *what* I heard, much less desiring to *do* anything about it. If there is anything to do, God will do it."

"I wrote it all down. Here it is..." I read the prophecies to him again.

Obviously disinterested, he pulled a file out of his desk drawer. "Are you finished? I have some work to do."

Frustrated and hurt, I walked upstairs and prepared for bed. Just before drifting off to sleep, the front door bell rang and the sound of familiar voices drifted up the stairs. I heard Jackie and Cappy. "Can we come in and talk to you, Ivan?"

I pulled on my robe and slipped down the stairs. The girls appeared relieved to see me, so I curled up in the living room chair.

Jackie bolted into the conversation in her usual all-or-nothing style. She didn't waste time with small talk about the price of tea in China or the warm

September evening. "There's something wrong in our congregation and God is angry."

Ivan leaned forward to listen. "Oh good," I thought. "At least he's listening to somebody."

"Something's going on here that's got to be straightened out." Jackie shared with sincere heart-felt concern while Cappy nodded in agreement. The girls continued on to describe a very personal situation involving members of our congregation which certainly violated Scriptural commandments.

Ivan allowed them to finish and then answered, "I hear what you're saying. But first, you don't have all the facts and I'm not free to discuss them with you. And second, we have no right to close the door of this church to anyone who comes to meet God — regardless of their personal circumstances. God will judge them — not me.

The discussion moved on. Jackie and Cappy refused to waver in their conviction that some kind of affirmative action was necessary. Ivan showed signs of frustration, but he tried to be pastoral and encouraged them to work with him within the congregation to raise the level of awareness regarding God's Word and holiness.

"Yes, the congregation does need to grow in its awareness of sin. We all do. The word we received tonight applies to each and every one of us in one way or another, and I can't withhold my ministry from those that fail. Don't forget the word about pride. Putting ourselves in judgment over the morality of others is a dangerous position to be in."

"But, what can we do?" Cappy asked again.

A Letter of Caution

"I'm doing everything that I feel I am called to do as the pastor of this congregation. If you feel strongly that you must act in some way, then I suggest you start with the leadership which God has placed here and share your feelings with them."

"Do you mean ... go to Church Council about this?"

Ivan leaned back slowly. This conversation showed definite signs of leading him into a very difficult position.

He could not tell them not to go to the Council, since the issue they raised could be decided there and only there. All decisions of membership and membership privileges rested ultimately with the Council. The pastor acted as the spiritual advisor.

Added to this, he'd worked long and hard to encourage a spirit of openness, encouraging everyone to approach council members with matters of concern.

However, this particular matter stirred quite a bit of unrest within my husband.

"You have the freedom to take anything you like to Council," he assured them slowly. "If you believe it's something you feel that you have to do."

The girls left, apparently feeling better. Ivan closed the door behind them and glared at me. "There's going to be trouble. I can smell it coming!"

A few days later Jackie telephoned, "Jean, Cappy's here and we're writing this letter for Council tonight. Listen and tell me how it sounds so far." She started to read, but instantly I received a check from the Holy Spirit: "Do not touch this."

"Jackie, I can't get involved in this one. I feel like the Lord is telling me to stay out of it."

"I know. I understand, but do you think we've said everything we want to say? Does it make sense?"

"It sounds ok."

"Does it make sense? Have we said what we want to say?"

"I guess so ... just keep praying about it."

Later in the day Jackie stopped by to pick up some Sunday School material and on her way out the kitchen door she reminded me, "This is only what Ivan told us to do."

I shrugged my shoulders. Yes, he did — kind of. However, I knew my husband well enough to know it was an answer like, "Sure, go jump off a bridge if that's what you really want to do."

I followed her out the door and called, "Remember, no matter what happens ... I still love you."

The next weeks and months evolved into a scrambled mess of "Who said that?"

"Who meant what?"

"Who did what?"

"Who sided with whom?"

And of course, "Who *really* heard from God?"

The original call to obey God's laws of holiness sank into a deep sea of misunderstanding and confusion.

Entire families joined the escalating battle. Everyone firmly stood his ground, convinced that the justice of God prevailed in his heart and mind.

My heart broke. My friendship with Jackie and Cappy lay on the altar of God. I shared their struggle. I heard the same call to holiness within my spirit.

But looking around I saw an institutional ministry filled with a mixed multitude, believers and non-believers alike, all with varying degrees of respect for

God's Word. It hurt me deeply to be a member of a denomination which accepted abortion by allowing "decisions of conscience," opened its pulpits to homosexual pastors, and neglected to confront sexual immorality.

Yet I understood my husband's responsibility to the denomination and his vows for ministry. I sympathized with his concern for those members who were unable to understand the importance of following God's commandments.

"I can preach, teach, and counsel God's Word, Jean. But I cannot enforce it in anyone's life. Each of our members remains free to choose or reject God's laws. Obedience must come from their hearts," he reminded me in no uncertain terms and with a look of determination. My pleas to understand Jackie and Cappy's motivation didn't sway him in the slightest.

Ivan's heart reached out to people where they stood in their walk with God. Tangled webs of sin and immorality aren't easily wound into a tidy ball of neat Christianity with one sermon or a few counseling sessions. One sin evolves into another and the endless downward spiral of sin and guilt pulls entire families into a whirlwind of spiritual deception.

Heartfelt conviction and repentance are, of course, the first steps to holiness. We must feel the conviction of the Holy Spirit. We must repent of our wicked ways and turn to righteousness.

But after we get up from our knees, decisions must be made. The process of putting away the past and beginning again is sometimes complicated.

My husband faced all of this and more in the

counseling room where he held fast to the conviction that decisions for God must come from the individual's heart — not from the counselor's tongue.

"Am I supposed to abandon those who fail to make an all-out decision to live the perfect Christian life?" he'd ask me.

"Is the Church supposed to close the door to everyone who lives a life of compromise? If it is, then I'll have to be the first one out the door because I know I'm not perfect yet."

"But aren't we supposed to stand for righteousness? Isn't the Church supposed to have standards?"

"Of course. But don't forget, the only standard we have is Jesus Christ Himself, and He's the One we are supposed to be pointing to — not at the faults of everyone who fails.

"Jean, you know that sanctification (a setting apart from sin) is an ongoing process. Just look how long it's taken you to come to the place you are now — and look how far you still have to go. And you expect these folks to transform their lives in a few days?"

He continued, "The Word of God and the Constitution of this Church outline standards of conduct for those in authority and leadership. The people in this situation are not in leadership and I believe they're doing everything possible to straighten out their lives. The Church Council is in agreement.

"What more do you want? If you want a congregation filled with holy saints, you'd better look somewhere else."

He gave me one of his looks that said, "I'm a little tired of this debate. Give it a rest, woman."

A Letter of Caution

Alone with God, I continued to wrestle. I believed the prophetic call to holiness. I also believed in my husband's ministry and his call to minister to the whole people of God, regardless of their spirituality. I stood over a growing chasm, one foot on either side, and it grew wider with each passing day.

"*Why, Lord?*"

In the stillness, only one word answered my prayer: "*Submit.*" As I received this word into my spirit, I reached for my husband's hand as he firmly pulled me to one side of the dividing chasm with him.

My Christian sisters stood on the other side. The storms of confusion and misunderstanding raged between us, but the Father's rainbow of promise touched both sides.

Cappy felt hurt and betrayed. She only wanted to follow Jesus. Hearing a call to holiness, she only wanted her church family to hear it too.

Jackie's anger flared. Her obedience to Jesus turned out to be very costly. Misunderstood by others, including her own pastor, she started to question this new path of spirituality she now walked. Growing pale and losing energy, one physical attack after another hit her. She resigned from Christian Education as the year ended, threatening, "It will be a long time before I do anything in this church again."

Ivan, torn by the strife himself, suffered from chest pain and after an intense physical the doctor warned him, "You're suffering from stress. You'd better start looking for another way to make a living or you're going to end up with a heart condition."

Warfare raged in our home. Annette, now nearly 17,

lived for only one purpose — to be out of our home and away from our "Christian rules." By attempting to legislate God's laws of holiness in our daughter's life we ended up driving her further and further away from us.

"Hypocrisy" screamed at us in our ministry and in our home. We professed a faith of love and unity in Christ, but failed at every turn.

Our songs stopped. Our joy disappeared.

"Jesus!" I cried, "What's happening? Our fellowship is falling apart. Is this the renewal You promised?"

"No, my daughter. This is *war*. My call to holiness is in your hearts. It is a *battle cry* coming forth to My people. I call you to live according to my Word.

"There's also an enemy at work in your hearts — his name is *Pride*. He turns you against one another in games of war. *I have a work to do. Let Me finish it.*"

From a depth I didn't even know existed within me, a song of lament poured forth in tears for a people I loved...

for my husband's ministry,

for a denomination I felt less and less a part of with each passing day,

and for myself, as I felt the heaviness of my Father's hand upon me.

Weep, oh weep Jerusalem, the judgment now begins —
Weep, oh weep Jerusalem, until the judgment ends.

A Letter of Caution 65

Jerusalem has stumbled and Judah fallen hard.
Her deeds and speech against the Lord
Defy His Holy Word.

Every man, his neighbor, feels oppression in the land:
Woe to those who fight the Lord
And choose to follow man.

(Isaiah 3)

His work continued until one by one, we fell on our knees before the Father and cried, "Lord, change me!"

With broken and contrite hearts we sang a song of repentance as we asked the Father to change us into the likeness of His Son. One voice followed another in a humble confession that we did not have all the answers.

Lord, change me, give me direction.
Lord, change me, take me by the hand.
I want to be a better Christian
And I know by Your help and understanding
that I can.

JG

We, in our small rural community, didn't face this battle alone. Throughout the Kingdom, from the great cathedrals to the small home fellowships, the call to live according to the Word of God issued forth in Scripture, in prophecy, in dreams and visions and through the voices of the prophets who spoke with trembling voices, as they sensed the seriousness of God's warnings.

They called us to holiness, to purity of thought,

word, and deed. Instead of examining our own hearts and lives, we misunderstood and turned on each other by waging games of war.

Brother against brother, sister against sister.

Our eyes focused on sin, not in ourselves, but in everyone else.

Congregations divided and renewal ministries splintered.

Christians scattered like frightened sheep.

Prominent religious leaders fell and will continue to fall as the root sin of *pride* is exposed before all — from the pulpit to the pew.

Pride: The enemy who fills our hearts with principles of Christianity, but dissuades us from living out these same principles by justifying our sinful thoughts and actions.

Pride: The enemy who gives us the desire to be vindicated of all wrong (be it in thought, word, or deed), to be known before all men as the one whom God has privately counseled and fought for, as the one who speaks untainted truth.

Pride: The enemy who forbids all change and growth in those around us, for he knows that he will be left behind. He justifies the one he abides in and points the all-condemning finger at all who oppose him.

Renewal ministries have taught us the lessons of spiritual warfare well. We have learned to take up the authority of Christ Jesus over the evil one.

We have learned to rebuke, renounce, and then to rejoice in the Name of Jesus. The captives are set free, the lame walk and the blind see. However, there is yet another lesson from the Father.

A Letter of Caution 67

Our pride will come under judgment, and judgment begins with the household of God.

We can't take authority over the judgment of God. We can't rebuke it. We can't cast it out.

It's essential for the Church to recognize the difference between the Father's discipline and demonic attack. Our spiritual ears must willingly hear His words of correction and loving rebuke.

He will put his finger of conviction upon our pride-filled lives; not our brother's life, not our sister's life — *our lives*. Yours and mine. *The walls of pride stand high and mighty.*

We do have a choice. We can fall before Him with hearts of repentance, or we can turn on each other to wage games of war for the delight of the evil one.

Yes, we'll continue to see sin abiding in the Body of Christ. We're gifted with spiritual sight and we see the difference between sin and righteousness.

We are to judge between good and evil.

We are to encourage each other in the way of righteousness. However, our brother's sin must become dim in comparison with our own. It's but a speck when we recognize the log of pride in our own eye.

Falling upon our knees in repentance for ourselves, a miracle takes place. From the inner chambers of our being, unadulterated prayer rises for Jesus to do a like work again and again in the hearts of His people. We pray with such intensity (in spirit and in truth) that the very stones (the hardened places inside of us) begin to cry out. We stand as true intercessors and weep for Jerusalem.

Holiness comes only one way — through the cross.

Unity comes only one way — through the cross.

The Father is sending us to the cross. There and only there will the enemy within us be defeated as we humble ourselves before God.

How many times have we played war games in the Body of Christ while the Father waited patiently for us to recognize the real enemy dwelling within us — the enemy attacking the Body of Christ at the very heart of its unity?

Yes, we play the game, pitting ourselves against one another, listening to the mocking voice of Pride, who coaches us from within.

The games go on day after day.

The tactics are unimportant.

The weapons count for little.

It's the one in whom Pride has the strongest hold who will claim success — it's the one who's able to endure the longest... to stand the tallest ... to continue to justify himself in the face of all arguments. Until, one day, someone stronger, someone bolder, and someone filled with an even greater spirit of pride will take it from him.

Or until he humbles himself under the hand of God and cries, "Lord, change me!"

Why is the Body of Christ broken and torn? Because we hear the call to holiness and then draw lines of battle to either enforce God's Word or, in some cases, to completely abandon it.

Why are fellowships which once testified to mighty works in the Name of Jesus now only memories? Because our members used the Name of Jesus and waved banners like spiritual fly-swatters against the enemy.

The first rule of warfare forgotten (identify your enemy), we batted aimlessly at anything and anyone suspected of sin. Yes, some turned out to be valid targets. Some turned out to be shadows of our imagination. But many turned out to be the people we loved the most.

And satan? He and his cohorts cheered us on for a most entertaining game.

Why have denominational renewal movements lost the powerful thrust they once enjoyed? Because we have attempted to rebuke the judgment of God for our denomination instead of accepting it and falling on our knees in repentance.

Why do Christians move from one fellowship to another, always searching for the home they never seem to find? I believe many Christians are restless and rootless because we hear Jesus calling His Church to holiness. Relentlessly, we search for a people to help us understand and live out the insistent call of God within our hearts.

Our prayer fellowship learned all of this and more through our Lord's classroom of obedience. We faced difficult truths one by one and allowed our lofty thoughts to fall to the ground.

Finally, the great battle with Pride was over — at least for a season. The war games were no longer played and had no winner of which to boast. Ivan continued to shepherd God's flock and minister to people at their level of faith, always encouraging them to reach higher, but never demanding it.

Jackie, Cappy, and I held out trembling arms and embraced each other again. It no longer mattered who was right and who was wrong. We stood together again in the Name of Jesus and the word of holiness continued to come forth as we prayed.

Our fellowship lay in fragmented pieces; broken vessels in the Potter's hand, waiting to be transformed into serving dishes, just as the earlier prophecy foretold.

He shaped us anew for ministry and in the distance we heard a new call — to praise His Name together, to share His love.

This time, however, something changed. A sense of separation started to grow between those who heard the call to holiness for their own lives and those who didn't.

It wasn't intentional. It wasn't judgmental. It simply happened. We found ourselves changing in the Potter's hands.

As a result, tensions rose between the call to follow His commandments and the institutional movement away from the authority of God's Word.

We loved our church. We prayed for the denomination. We tried to speak out, but our voices were silenced by the voices of men in authority over us.

We didn't want to engage in games of war again, and thus we remained silent as the church we knew and loved slowly moved in opposition to the Word of God.

I watched my husband, torn between his call to minister as an institutional pastor to a mixed multitude and his call to minister the uncompromising Word of God to a people who stand willing to accept the call of holiness in their own lives.

They are both from God, but how long would he be able to bear the burden? *"How long, Lord?"*

A Letter of Caution

In our fellowship we lifted our voices and the Holy Spirit filled us with new songs of intercession.

For Zion's sake, send forth the battle cry,
Jerusalem, lift high the trumpet sound.
His victory we'll be and His unity we'll see
When we're living here according to God's Word.

Call your people forth to praise Your Name
Call us Lord, we won't be put to shame
Sound the trumpet call, yes, call us one
  and all
To live Your Word and witness to its power.

Today, the seed of this vision grows within all of us. Ivan and I look longingly to the future. Someday, somewhere, we will live together according to His Word. Those who stumble in sin will be helped to their feet by strong, loving Christians who refuse to play war games of pride. We'll be one body, each having weaknesses and strengths, supporting one another and unashamedly asking for help in Jesus' Name.

The Father is building His Church without the walls of division and pride. The people of this Church are going to walk in holiness, separated unto God — not because of legalistic teachings, but because we hear the Father say, "Be not afraid to hear the battle cry for holiness!"

The walls of pride are coming down in the Name of Jesus!

Suggested Scripture Meditation: Jeremiah 13:15-17
                                  Jeremiah 18:5-6
                                  Isaiah 62

Chapter Three

A Letter of Inner Healing to Those Who Hear the Shepherd's Call

"Be not afraid to walk in the valley with Me."

As long as warfare continues, wounded soldiers and casualty lists will abound. Whether in war games or critical confrontations with the powers of darkness, we spend ourselves in the fight.

Everywhere I travel in the Body of Christ, I encounter painful reminders of the battlefield.

It's in your eyes.

It's in your voice.

I sense your battered spirit because I've traveled the same path and walked through the land mines of hidden agendas (manipulative plans of others — often disguised with soft-sounding words). These words explode in front of us and fill our lives with painful fragments of sharp, cutting pieces of verbiage and emotion.

Our friends are brought to the ground by the flaming arrows of the evil one. Spiritual babes are caught up in controversy as deadly as chemical warfare.

And yes, I know what it's like to be seen as the "enemy."

The ravages of spiritual warfare clutter the highways and byways of Christianity with broken hearts and discouraged pilgrims. Day after day these pilgrims are passed over by well-meaning ministers of the Gospel who have no time in their busy schedules for such ministry. But the Holy Spirit will not pass us by. He wants to pour healing ointment on our wounds and bind up our broken hearts.

I remember my first weak steps as a Christian and the long hours of prayer offered in my behalf by loving Spirit-filled Christians. I needed healing deep within.

I needed revelation gifts to open buried wounds and forgiveness to cover them. I needed the restoration ministry of the Holy Spirit to give me the strength to go on. *I needed, I needed, and I needed.*

I am so thankful for those who took the time to give in the Name of Jesus.

Today, many years later, ministry is multiplied many times over for everyone. Even those of us who want to take the time to patiently minister gifts of inner healing don't have enough hours in the day to touch all the hands reaching out to us. Too many battlefields are scattered with wounded warriors.

Jesus knows this time is upon us. He sees the pain and hears the prayers streaming forth from the brokenhearted. He hears the cries of yesterday, and today,

76 A Church Without Walls

and even those we are going to utter in the morning. Time belongs to Him.

He wants to heal us and give us strength to go on. He sends His Holy Spirit to speak words of comfort and healing. The Spirit speaks, but we must take the time to *listen,* to *receive,* and to *understand* this work!

We're facing difficult days. Each day the coming of our Lord draws closer and the evil one mounts his forces against the Body of Christ.

We must be healthy and strong in body, mind, and spirit. We have to throw away our emotional crutches and walk in the Spirit with steps of conviction and purpose!

How shall we achieve this? By *listening* to the voice of Jesus as He bids us to walk with Him in the valley for inner healing and restoration.

By allowing the healing ministry of the Holy Spirit to reveal our wounds to us, to heal us, and to show us how to walk in love.

It's a walk of solitude. One place I must travel alone.

I know when the time arrives. The difficult circumstances of yesterday press in upon me. Past conversations play over and over again and the high mountain of God appears insurmountable. I want to dance and sing in the City of Zion, but first I must pass through the Valley Gate (Neh. 2:15) to enter Jerusalem.

Come, take a valley walk. Give each concern, one by one, to your Shepherd. Forgive and receive forgiveness in Jesus' Name. Take the time to stop, to pray, to reflect upon the painful areas in your life which need a touch from God.

I don't believe in special techniques or formulas for

A Letter of Inner Healing 77

inner healing. It's the presence of Jesus Himself, revealing, touching, and restoring a willing and submissive heart.

The small experience which follows is but a shadow of the work He wants to do in all of us. The footsteps I ask you to take with me are quiet ones. If you listen carefully, you'll hear the gentle song of the Shepherd.

Do you have a valley deep down inside of you,
  of fear, disappointments and pain?
Are you walking through memories day after day,
  finding your footsteps the same?

Yes, I heal the memories of yesterday's pain,
  and I go where no man can go.
No longer you'll walk in dark valleys alone.
  I'm with you wherever you go.

Today, or tomorrow, even yesterday's pain —
  yes, I'm the Lord of them all.
The light of my love will shine forth like the sun
  wherever dark shadows may fall.

Jesus gently reminds us again, "I am able."

The choice, however, remains ours. We're free to remain in our present state, or to accept His offer in simple faith.

Lord Jesus, walk through this valley with me,
  cleanse me and make me whole.
You are my Shepherd, I won't be afraid,
  Your love is restoring my soul.

The winter storms had raged not only through the skies, but through our congregation and our homes.

Relationships still lay in broken pieces, casualties of the war games we played.

At home Annette continued to resist the disciplines and expectations of a Christian home. The faith she knew and loved as a child now represented a prison of "unjust claims" upon her life.

Karen, sixteen, excelled in everything she touched academically, but at home she watched her sister slowly turn into someone she didn't know. She felt the pain of losing someone very special in her life.

Five-year-old Mark simply absorbed the fulness of life around him and, at times, the pain of a home divided.

Ivan considered potential calls from other congregations. His heart ached for a spiritual freedom he couldn't find here. Yet God refused to release him from his ministry in this place.

Spring. A time of new beginnings,
new expectations,
new growth.
Oh yes! Thank You, Jesus!

But first, I needed time to put away the pain of yesterday. I needed to spend time with my Lord.

Linda (now a dear friend and prayer partner) also shared a similar need. Her ministry of intercession sent her into the heat of spiritual warfare for the sake of God's people. She needed a time to be alone, to regroup, to touch the heart of God.

"Jean," Linda shared one afternoon, "I know Jesus wants me to take two days for prayer and fasting. It keeps coming back and I'm putting it off. I just don't know how I'll ever manage it at home with the kids, and the phone — and the food!"

A Letter of Inner Healing   79

"You need, I need. Let's go away for a couple of days. If we share expenses it won't cost much," I suggested.

Within the month we embarked on our two-day retreat of silence and prayer at a Christian retreat center in the mountains.

Without any agenda of our own, we prayerfully handed ourselves and our time over to our Shepherd. Although we shared a common room, once our retreat began we moved independently of each other and we maintained a vow of silence.

Bible and notebook in hand on our first evening, I settled down by the window and waited. With a smile I remembered all the pleas I'd lifted up to heaven for "some peace and quiet."

Now, here I was.

Eventually, the rush of mental activity slowed down and I slipped into a oneness with the silence around me.

> My soul waits in silence for God only,
> For my hope is from Him.
> For He only is my rock and my salvation,
> My stronghold; I shall not be shaken.
> On God my salvation and my glory rest;
> The rock of my strength, my refuge is in God.
> Trust in Him at all times, O people;
> Pour out your heart before Him;
> God is a refuge for us.
>
> Psalm 62:5-8

I thumbed through the Scriptures, instinctively looking for something ... but what?

Exactly where did Jesus want to take me on this pilgrimage?

What did He want me to discover about myself? What did I need from Him?

Suddenly, all my preconceived ideas about what might or might not happen during this time vanished like lifeless vapors.

In their place a very subtle feeling stirred me. My thoughts formulated into one word.

"Love."

"Yes, Lord?"

"Love."

"Yes Lord, but what about it?"

"Love."

One word. Nothing else. Just that one small word. I opened my Bible and researched dozens of Scriptures about love, carefully writing the significant ones in my prayer diary.

The pages filled and the hours passed.

Linda returned from her walk and the darkness outside forced the two of us together in our room. Without making eye contact, unless by accident, we continued the vow of silence through the rest of the night.

As I drifted off to sleep that evening a tinge of guilt nudged me. It felt awkward and unnatural not to speak or communicate in some fashion, as if we violated sacred laws of friendship.

Many hours later my eyes opened to the first light of morning and a flutter of excitement filled my thoughts. "The whole day — just for You, Jesus!"

Linda and I snuck a quick "good-morning" smile at each other, but one smile said both "good-morning" and "good-bye" at the same time. Each of us moved to the call of our Shepherd.

I walked out into the morning air. I'm not an avid nature lover at heart. I enjoy the outdoors, but give me a cozy chair, climate control, modern conveniences, and I'm a happy camper!

However, a new sense of belonging to my Heavenly Father's world filled me on this particular morning. Indeed, I felt at home here in the midst of His creation. A song Jesus gave to Jackie, *God Created the World*, played over and over again in my mind.

I considered the trees growing tall and strong under the Father's eye, and how my life compared to those trees — passing through seasons, enduring storms, continually growing in spite of the children who attacked them with imaginary weapons and the dogs who used them to mark their territory.

The well-worn picnic tables and dusty barbecue pits reminded me of people, of laughter, and of voices calling out to each other. Serving in ministry had gifted Ivan and me with such a large, wonderful family. After all our years in so many places, I enjoyed the sense of community and belonging.

Unexpectedly, the pain of betrayal flashed through me like a lightening bolt. Memories of recent congregational misunderstandings and verbal assaults welled up and out their hiding places in my subconscious.

Voices!
Faces!
Accusations!
Pain!
Confusion!

Memories flashed, one after the other, set to the music of angry cymbals and the devil's laughter.

The recent conflict certainly wasn't the first one since the beginning of our ministry, but this time it involved so many of those whom I trusted ... and they trusted me. I stood both as the betrayer and the betrayed.

How could it happen?
In a church?
In the family of God?

> It is not an enemy who taunts me —
> then I could bear it;
> it is not an adversary who deals
> insolently with me —
> Then I could hide from him,
> But it is you, my equal, my companion,
> my familiar friend.
> We used to hold sweet converse together;
> Within God's house we walked in fellowship.
> Psalm 55:12-14a

Kneeling beside a small stream, I watched the clear water run over and through the rocks, fallen leaves, and the forest debris. If I lifted a handful of forest residue from the stream bed, I'd have a handful of rotting muck.

I felt like muck. Painful memories, just lying there beneath the surface of my life, waiting for the process of time to disintegrate them.

"Oh, Jesus, if I allow you to lift those memories up from their hiding place, can I bear the stench?"

As if in answer to my tumbling prayers, I glanced up and watched the sun filter down through the tangled tree limbs and onto the water. As I continued to watch the sun rays, Jesus started to send the healing light of

His love through the tangled branches of my own life.
The heavens didn't open.
The earth didn't shake.
I simply felt His gentle presence and I allowed Him to speak to my heart through the scene unfolding in front of me. His light rested upon the "muck" of my past experiences.

In Him there is no darkness — no muck — and as the sun continued to shine on the water and the debris beneath it disappeared from view, so His Holy Spirit dispelled the darkness from my unpleasant memories.

Simply, I let go of the past. No longer holding onto resentments and hurtful feelings of yesterday, I forgave and received forgiveness in Jesus' Name. I acknowledged my sin before Him and He forgave me all my iniquities. My own confession of sin released me to forgive others.

A basic revelation of sin.
An uncomplicated act of my will.
A touch of God's forgiveness.

I felt my sisters' pain as well as my own. Jackie, Cappy, and others ... they hurt. They felt the pain of betrayal and misunderstanding emanating from my words and actions, regardless of my "good intentions."

All of us — victims of our own pride, separated from each other by walls of our own making.

Unlike some of my past experiences with inner healing (involving varying degrees of emotional response), I felt no rush of emotion, no tears — just a simple acceptance of a Divine work taking place inside of me.

It was as simple as breathing out the poisonous gases

of unforgiveness and breathing in the fresh air of God's grace. Yet it was equally as complicated as life itself and as mysterious as the atoning work of Jesus Christ on the cross and the shedding of His blood for you and for me.

I stood up and took a deep breath. The past remained unchanged, just as the stream bed at my feet remained intact, but the memory of it didn't hurt anymore.

It's difficult to explain the absence of pain in a once painful memory. The past is unchanged, but I'm no longer consumed with an emotional response to the events, nor am I in bondage to these emotions.

My sinful responses are on the cross and by His stripes I am healed — within. A miracle of inner healing has transpired.

Throughout the day my valley walk continued. Shadows fell across the wooded path and resurrected deep-seated fears.

Sunbeams reflected dreams and visions, some fulfilled and others still hoped for. Wherever I stepped on this pilgrimage of silence, God spoke; He touched; He restored.

Jesus touched my inner man quietly and gently, almost as if my simple act of obedience in coming to this place released healing for my tired spirit.

Our physical bodies tire and we rest. Too often Christians treat spiritual weariness and disease with more activities, more rigorous Bible studies, more hours of praise and worship. They're all very important and very good for us — but sometimes we need to learn how to *rest our spirits* by simply *abiding in Him and allowing the Holy Spirit to minister to us.*

A Letter of Inner Healing

Many will debate that inner healing is nothing more than repentance and forgiveness. In one sense, I agree. However, there is a supernatural element of revelation knowledge present in the ministry of inner healing.

We need the revelation gifts of the Holy Spirit to pinpoint specific areas in our lives standing in need of such healing.

Added to this we need to *listen* to the Holy Spirit as He speaks words of forgiveness to us.

By the time evening fell on our second day, I no longer wanted to speak to Linda. Out of love, I wanted her to have the same gift she gave to me — time with her Lord.

Love — we think we have it all together. Then God breaks in. He shows us still another dimension of His love for us and gifts us to translate this same love to others.

If I loved someone or something, be it family, friend, or even possessions, I wanted to hold them close. I loved with a jealous love.

I don't believe these responses are entirely wrong, since Jesus loves us jealously and He wants to keep us very close to Him. However, my love needed balance. The love Jesus has for us *holds us tightly in the palm of His Hand and at the same time sets us free.*

This inner work of forgiveness and healing touched me at the very foundation of all my relationships. In the coming days, weeks, and months, I'd experience the gift of love in a new way.

Love is letting go and giving others the freedom to choose...

to be successful or to make mistakes...

to stretch their wings of faith and learn to fly, even when learning might include falling.

Again, no dramatic experience.

Loving, letting go, and letting God be God to those I love.

A quiet work, ordained by my Lord, and by His stripes I am healed.

The next morning greeted me with a sense of sadness. In a few short hours we'd have to leave this place of solitude. Selfishly, I wanted to stay just a little longer.

Every moment was designed just for me, for my needs, my healing, my relationship with Jesus. I was accountable to no one but God. Oh, just to stay in the valley with Jesus!

Up and dressed, Linda moved slowly to the bathroom for another drink of water. Following her covenant with the Lord, she continued to fast, drinking only water and sips of orange juice.

(I didn't embark on a fast, but took small amounts of food in the retreat's kitchen to control a border-line diabetic condition.)

A deep sigh following the sound of running water in the bathroom jerked me back to reality...Linda didn't feel well!

Instinctively, I wanted to reach out... to take care of her. She walked back into the room and I shot her a concerned look. I grabbed a tablet and scribbled a quick note asking, "Are you all right?"

Her smile answered "Yes," but her slow unsteady steps cried out, "Help me, Jesus!"

I threw back the covers. I needed to get on with life —

to love and be loved, to minister and be ministered to.

The compassion welling up inside of me for Linda reignited my desire for oneness with my family and God's family — to begin anew with a fresh commitment to keep on "keeping on."

"Forgive me, Lord, for my selfishness. You've created me to need others and to be needed by them. I can't stay in the valley."

At home, a panorama of life waited for me, just as one is waiting for you. The infilling of love I received from my Lord promised to see me through the sunshine and rain of the coming months.

In a few days I'd experience the pain of watching Annette leave our home on her seventeenth birthday. And I would love her in spite of the pain. I loved her with a new love — a love which gave her the freedom to choose.

She traveled a separate road of life. We had no choice. Although we wanted to, legally we couldn't force her to stay. The Holy Spirit instructed us, "Let her go. I will be her parent."

Jesus also knew about the joy He planned for us. He could see Karen reaching out for and receiving a dramatic healing of scoliosis as we opened our home and ministry to a traveling evangelist.

He knew about a word of knowledge from the 700 Club television ministry and the healing of Mark's long-term food allergies.

All this and more. Jesus knew. Taking me by the hand, He led me up and out of the valley, to face tomorrow unafraid.

Understanding the Valley Experience from the Perspective of God's Word

Psalm 23 — The purpose of the valley is restoration. "He restores my soul."

We need our Shepherd (Jesus) to lead us in the valley. It isn't safe to walk through the valley alone. Satan will come and attack us at our weakest point, attempting to drive us into a dark ravine of emotional entrapment filled with self-pity and despair. Depression is the name of satan's valley walk. "The Lord is my shepherd ... I fear no evil for thou art with me."

Death takes place in the valley. "I walk through the valley of the shadow of death." We're prepared to die to self, and to many of the expectations we place on ourselves, others, and God.

First Kings 20:28 — Jesus is the Lord of the valley who proves Himself against the enemies which rise up against us, the enemies of fear, betrayal, misunderstanding, failure, loneliness, etc.

Ezekiel 37:1-14 — His Spirit breathes new life in the valley, into our physical frames which are burdened and weighed down with anxiety, to our bones which are dry from discouraging words. "Anxiety in a man's heart weighs him down, but a good word makes him glad" (Prov. 12:25).
"A cheerful heart is good medicine, but a downcast spirit dries up the bones" (Prov. 17:22).

Solomon 2:1 — He is the lily of the valley. He opens our eyes to His creative wonders in the valley. Our feet walk upon a path lined with the handiwork of our Father. All of this is our Father's world — our home. We are loved and secure.

First John 1:5-9 — He's the Light in the valley. As we walk in the light of His love, His blood cleanses us from all sin. There is no room for darkness where His light shines.

Hebrews 13:8 — He is Lord of Time in the valley. He is the same, yesterday, today and tomorrow. He reaches into our past, our today, and our tomorrows with His love. He heals, restores, and prepares.

Our Responsibility in the Valley

Psalm 23 — Our responsibility is to be still and to wait for the Shepherd. We must accept the discipline of silence before God and accept the valley experience for what it is — a time for reflection and healing. We may walk in the valley at a secluded retreat setting or in the midst of everyday activity. Our valley may take place during a few moments of prayer or during hours or days. Wherever we are, it is imperative for us to give Jesus the time to lead us beside the still waters.

I must decide to forgive both others and myself. When I do, I'm ready to accept the forgiveness of God.

I agree to willingly leave the valley at the appointed time. Too many of us want to set up tents in the valley, to live among the flowers in solitude with Jesus, away from the demands of ministry. Far too many of God's people, wounded from brutal church battles, have chosen to actually *live* in the valley. Unwilling to risk again, they want to remain uninvolved, noncommitted, and aloof from Body ministry.

The Father is sending forth a song, calling us to accept the valley for what it is and to move on. There is more waiting for His Church — much more!

His Church without walls will consist of Christians

who have walked in the valley, received healing and are willing to return to the Body of Christ with open arms. This Church will not allow the Body of Christ to die on the battlefield of spiritual warfare!

Healed, we are rising up in the Name of Jesus! *The inner walls of painful memories and disappointments are coming down!*

Restored, He is sending us out, back to the Body to climb a new mountain of faith rising before us.

Chapter Four

A Letter of Faith to Those Who Desire to See Miracles in Their Lives

"Be not afraid to reach for a miracle!"

We simply refused to believe it. Marie's words sounded like the dialog from a television program — not her life.

"The doctor says I have cancer."

Marie loved to talk about Jesus. She told everyone how He had saved her and how He would save this person or that person if we'd just keep praying and refuse to give up.

Her children and grandchildren filled her life, but she found plenty of time to visit the sick, the shut-ins, and the nursing homes. She sang in the choir, taught Sunday school, and supported nearly every activity in our congregation.

Time passed. Marie walked in confident trust —

A Letter of Faith   93

Jesus was going to heal her. We too believed for her healing. Jackie reminded me, "If *anybody's* going to be healed, it will be Marie."

Treatments, pain, and prayer followed our sister wherever she went. "It's in the bone," she reported matter-of-factly. So we stepped up our prayers of faith and confessed her healing.

Marie arrived at the parsonage one Wednesday morning for Bible Study with jubilant praise, "My X-ray shows new bone growth! The doctor calls it a miracle! Praise the Lord!

Time continued to pass, however, and the pain within her body increased. The endless merry-go-round of medications, treatments, and tests almost seemed to cooperate with the deadly disease inside of her by draining her physical strength and endurance. Marie wanted to talk about dying, but we didn't let her.

"Jesus is going to heal you," I reminded her.

"Jesus *has* healed you!" Cindy stated emphatically. "Receive it and thank Him for it!"

"Yes, yes He has. I know that ... it's just that sometimes it's so hard to have the faith I know I'm supposed to have."

Ivan watched and listened. He shared God's Word with her and reminded her, "Keep your eyes on Jesus, Marie, not the doctors. They are only instruments in His hands. Jesus is the Great Physician."

Medical reports worsened and so did Marie's strength. Eventually, hospitalization for short periods turned into a common occurrence. But we kept praying, never letting go and always believing for

94 A Church Without Walls

God's healing — until Marie died, peacefully, with her family gathered around her bedside.

Why, Lord?

A young husband and father in our congregation, vibrant and full of life. Diagnosis: Cancer. We prayed, we believed, we trusted God.

One night Jackie telephoned me. "Jean, can you come over? I just received a new song from the Lord."

"Praise God! What's it like?"

"I'm not so sure. You'd better come listen."

After she sang it for me, we stared at the words of the song, hastily written in Jackie's handwriting on the pages of her prayer diary. Although beautiful and filled with promise, an undeniable sense of sadness overshadowed the quiet tune. One note rolled into the other with a feeling of inevitable destiny.

For every time, there is a season
It is all part of God's great plan.
We need to trust, love and obey Him
Even for the times when we don't understand.

Days aren't always full of sunshine
Some times heavy rains must fall;
But rainbows are signs of God's promise
That He'll be here to help us stand tall.

JG

The next day Bob died.

Why, Lord?

During the same year, Ivan's step-father consulted the doctor for a painful arthritic limp. A routine X-ray report revealed cancer. Before the year ended, despite surgery, medication, treatments, and many prayers, my mother-in-law buried her second husband.

A Letter of Faith

Why, Lord?

Joan, my dear friend, wrote to me, "They've found cancer in my breast. I've had a mastectomy and I'm now on chemotherapy, trusting the Lord for a total healing."

Five years later the cancer returned. More surgery. More treatments. More pain. Joan's fight against death continued until one day she died.

Why, Lord?

My husband and I sat in the surgeon's office two weeks after my breast biopsy. It was a routine procedure after my mammogram revealed minute calcifications.

"Mrs. Koberlein, there's not going to be any easy way to explain this to you. You have a rare form of early breast cancer."

I listened quietly, perfectly confident that whatever was wrong could be easily corrected. After all, he had said "early." The doctor continued.

"Before I say anything, I want you to know that the condition your lab reports show is a very controversial issue in medicine today. I've requested biopsy reports from the top cancer people. I don't want any mistakes to be made here."

He continued, describing multiple lab reports from the major cancer hospitals. It started to sink in. This wasn't routine. The word "early" didn't appear to carry as much weight as I'd first thought. Something "big" was about to come down.

"At this point the cells are noninvasive. They aren't spreading to other cells or moving to other parts of your body.

"There is a chance that we removed all the malignant

cells during the biopsy. There is also a 30% chance that it will return in one or both of your breasts. *We just don't know.*

"Surgery is the only medical option I can offer you, Mrs. Koberlein ... the removal of one or, to be completely safe, both of your breasts. At this time there is no other medical option. Chemotherapy and radiation treatment are not considered effective for this type of cancer."

I heard his words. I understood, or at least I thought I understood. But I couldn't react with any sense of emotion because my mind fought desperately to turn back time; to wipe these moments out of my life and to go on without them.

Completely in control, I continued to listen, certain that at any moment it would all go away.

"There is another option," he continued. "As I explained, there's much controversy over this form of cancer. You may choose a very conservative approach: not to have the surgery, to submit to frequent mammograms and examinations, and a future of multiple biopsies to determine whether or not the disease actually returns.

"This is an option with a high degree of risk. The disease may return or become invasive at any point. Many women are not prepared to live with this risk.

"The decision is yours. I want you to take some time to think about it. Get some other opinions, consider the alternatives, think about the risk you're able to live with, and let me know what you decide."

After nearly an hour of explanations, questions, medical terminology, and the statistics foretelling my chances of future survival, Ivan and I walked out of his office. Time failed to reverse itself and the dam of emotions building up inside me started to break through my trembling body.

Choking the tears down, I looked ahead to the future. A stack of medical papers with my name on them placed a sentence of death upon me. A curse from satan himself held me tightly in its grip.

My doctor promised no miracles. He confessed the inadequacies of the medical profession's ability to guarantee a total cure. "This form of cancer scatters itself instead of forming tumors. The cells may or may not scatter. They may or may not become invasive. *We just don't know.*

"Many women live their entire lifetime with these noninvasive cancer cells and never develop a full-blown cancer. *We just don't know* what will happen your particular case.

"There's also the possibility that the biopsy procedure has completely removed the problem area and you're totally cured. *We just don't know.*"

I felt fragile, ready to shatter into a thousand pieces and die. I'd been cheated — it wasn't fair. It didn't make sense. I was thirty-eight years old and experiencing the healthiest years of my life.

We stepped into the elevator. Ivan moved to put his arm around me. "Hey there, it's not the end of the world..."

I pulled away. For an instant I hated him. My world did end; at least, the one I knew and loved.

Very simply, I went home and started to die. I gave in to the curse. I believed the lie of the enemy. The *fear of cancer* drained every ounce of my physical strength. Walking the flight of stairs to our second floor proved impossible without stopping to rest midway.

The pain from my biopsy incision, almost nonexistent to this point, now intensified, and every small movement reminded me of the enemy trying to claim my life, a silent time bomb ready to explode inside of me at any given moment. Did I have three years, five years, ten years? How long?

During those first few days I lashed out at my husband. I accused him of not caring and threatened, "If I die, it'll be because you aren't praying hard enough!"

I'd attack, cry, and fall into his waiting arms. I needed someone to blame, someone to be angry at. I needed some way to attack because I hurt so deeply. I wanted to fight back — but how?

"Help me, Jesus!"

We started the round of surgeons. I wanted to go to the City of Faith in Tulsa, Oklahoma. Without a question, Ivan picked up the phone to start making plane reservations.

"Whichever path you choose, Jean," he advised me again and again, "you must go all the way with it. If you follow the medical procedures, then you must be prepared to submit to everything they prescribe and trust God through them. If you choose the path of trusting God for healing without surgery, then you must be prepared to take every step, regardless of how difficult the path becomes."

"Maybe Jesus wants me to have the surgery. Maybe that's His plan for my healing?" I'd ask Ivan, wanting him to make the decision for me.

"Maybe He does. But this is something that only you're going to know — it's your body. I'll support you and love you; but this decision is yours, Jean. I won't make it for you."

My dilemma remained. Which path did Jesus want me to take?

Healing wasn't the question. *I knew Jesus wanted to heal me.* How to *cooperate with Him in the healing process* was another question. Jesus uses medicine. He also performs miracles, some instantly and some progressively.

The path of healing always seemed so simple before: Pray, trust God, listen to medical advice, expect and receive your healing!

But now the doctors placed a decision in my hands. Ivan placed a decision in my hands. No one would make it for me. I had to decide. I needed to hear from God. I needed to hear His voice as never before. Only in hearing His instruction and walking in obedience could I break the curse and defeat the enemy. I needed to hear! And I heard ... nothing.

I wrestled with my motives. Yes, I wanted to keep my body intact, to keep from losing so much of my physical identity as a woman. Yes, volatile emotions erupted inside of me like an explosive volcano.

Yet underneath, an even greater surge of emotion rushed. I wanted to defeat the enemy, to break the curse of death. And I vowed to do whatever necessary to do this. If surgery — so be it!

In many respects I relived the days leading up to my deliverance from the occult, once again facing a powerful enemy dwelling inside of me — an enemy calling for my death. My freedom rested in the power of Jesus!

I wanted to fight in His Name! I experienced victory at my deliverance from occult bondage. Yes! I'd experience it again!

Following the scriptural command of James 5:14, "Is anyone among you sick? Let him call for the elders of the church, and let them pray over him, anointing him with oil in the Name of our Lord; and the prayer offered in faith will restore the one who is sick, and the Lord will raise him up," Ivan and I asked our Church Council to come to the church to anoint me with oil, lay hands upon me, and pray for my healing. Although this proved to be a new experience for the majority of them, they came. And they prayed.

During our time together in the sanctuary, the presence of God enveloped me with a new sense of His love. Underneath the power of these prayers, I felt a greater protection, a greater sense of security, and a greater peace than I'd known since that afternoon in the surgeon's office.

Their prayers wrapped me up in a blanket of love and concern. I felt like a small child tucked into bed at night. You know what it feels like: safe, secure. The darkness is still there, but it's all right because it is safe and warm under the covers.

"Does this mean you've made a decision?" Ivan asked when I explained my feelings to him later.

"No, it just means I'm not afraid of the decision any longer."

One step at a time, the Holy Spirit gently led me. In faith I looked back over the past year, remembering dreams, visions, and special words from the Lord, preparing me for all of this, saying, "This is the way, walk ye in it."

The doctor had shown me the X-ray which justified the biopsy procedure. The area of concern, microcalcifications, were noted circled in small broken lines by the doctor.

In a dream, months earlier, I'd seen that very same picture, and a voice in the dream cautioned me, "It's growing larger."

On three separate occasions during the previous year, as I prayed with friends, God spoke through the gift of visions. All three visions, two from Diane and one from a dear pastoral friend, showed me standing at a crossroad, suitcase packed, trying to decide which way to go.

The Sunday before I received my final lab reports, I stood with our church choir and sang an anthem from Psalm 91. The words rang out with the authority of prophecy and spoke deeply to my heart, *"A thousand may fall at my side, ten thousand at my right hand, but it will not come near me..."*

Yes, Jesus stood with me in this, preparing me, protecting me, and now directing me. "Oh Jesus, give me the wisdom to *understand* what You're trying to tell me."

During our visit to the City of Faith we visited the Journey Through the Bible in the Healing Outreach Center, a dramatized walk-through of the Bible. There, in the final prayer room, listening to a recorded prayer for healing, I actually felt the presence of *something heavy* lift up and out of me.

Unknown to Ivan and me, our congregation gathered in prayer for me during our trip to Tulsa. Scriptures and visions received by various members of the congregation confirmed God's hand upon my life.

After we arrived back home, during our monthly Women's Aglow Meeting, a strange sensation occurred randomly throughout the evening — small bursts of coolness radiated from several areas of my breasts.

After the meeting Cindy shared with me, "Jean, I was praying for you so hard, and I saw these strange 'popping' pictures, as if God caused something to explode!"

Dreams, visions, Scriptures, encouraging words from friends, long hours of prayer searching for God's heart; yet still I had no definite answer.

Three surgeons counseled me, "Do not delay. Have the surgery immediately." (Added to his counsel, one surgeon remarked honestly, "If I do not counsel you in this way, I will open myself to a lawsuit.")

Only one man, my original doctor, said, "Jean, you have a choice to make. No one can make it for you."

"Which way, Lord, which way?"

Shortly after we returned from Tulsa, Ivan's schedule called for a two-week trip to Michigan for a Bible study training series. He didn't want to leave me, but I insisted.

"Go, I'll be fine."

And I was, until I turned on the 700 Club to hear Pat Robertson telling about his wife Dede's mastectomy. I listened, frozen and trembling. Thoughts raced through my mind. Who do I think I am? If Dede Robertson wasn't healed, what do I think I'm doing? I'm playing a game with death.

"Oh, Jesus!" I cried out in panic, *"What do You want me to do! What! I can't put this off any longer. I have to know. Tell me what to do and I'll do it. I'll have the surgery if you want me to. What? Jesus! What?"*

My eyes still wet with tears, and Pat Robertson still

challenging every woman to have a mammogram, the telephone rang.

It was my doctor. "Jean, I've been waiting to hear from you. What have you decided?"

In the flashing moments between his question and my answer, *I knew*. Of all the people to call, he was the only surgeon who was prepared to support and follow my case without surgical intervention. Had any of the other doctors phoned, or even a concerned friend watching the 700 Club, I would have moved in the direction of surgery.

Even the absence of a call would have pushed me in that direction. Dede's experience with breast cancer certainly advocated immediate surgery.

In a calm voice, with an inner strength that surprised even me, I replied, "I'm going to wait, to take the conservative approach you described and have regular examinations."

Without a word of reproach he accepted my answer with a firm, "Then let's set up your next appointment and get started. We're going to keep a real close eye on you."

After agreeing on the appointment date, I put the receiver down and whispered, "Thank You, Jesus," very much aware that I'd received this phone call by Divine appointment.

My mouth repeatedly confessed my faith as it rose from deep inside my spirit. However, every day I continued to stand at the crossroads, to question my decision, to go back over the medical reports, the conversations, the prayers, the dreams, the counsel of so many, and the promises in God's Word.

I found it impossible to move from the dilemma of mental reasoning. Back and forth, from one line of defense to another, weighing the implications and risks of each decision, questioning my motives, my priorities in life, and even the value of life itself.

I wanted to hear a simple promise from Jesus. "You're healed! It's all over." I ached for those simple words to resound through my spirit with a loud voice, or even in a still small voice. But they never came.

To make the situation even more difficult, I knew that a medical confirmation of healing was impossible. Only my death, of causes other than breast cancer, could ever verify a healing.

Cancer cells often lie undetected within the body for years and years. The eye of God alone could see inside my body and proclaim healing. I wanted desperately to hear this proclamation from Jesus.

Instead, during one of our Wednesday night Bible Studies, an answer I didn't expect broke through the silence in my heart. As the group prayed for me I sensed the strong presence of Jesus, and His Holy Spirit spoke with a loving, yet firm statement of fact.

"It's not which path is right or wrong, My daughter. Whom do you trust? Where does your faith rest? The decision is yours. I will be with you on either path."

Again, I stood at the crossroad, but this time with new spiritual sight. It wasn't the *decision itself* which was right or wrong — but rather, where did I see *my trust in Jesus?*

On the path of surgery was an enemy which haunted me day and night — *fear*. It stood waiting for me in an angry cloud of dark shadows, thundering the words of all the doctors we'd talked to. *"We don't know ...We just don't know!"*

On the next path I saw Jesus, *who did know* what the doctors confessed to not knowing. He knew about the changes taking place within my body before any X-ray or lab report told the doctors.

I saw Jesus, who in His love and in His time revealed the cancerous cells and arranged for them to be removed in time.

I saw Jesus ... and a peaceful light holding no shadows, no secrets. He knows all, sees all, understands all, and He is the Great Physician.

Another woman might stand at the same crossroad of decision and see Jesus standing on the path of surgery, dependent upon what is taking place deep inside her spirit. *The choice is not right or wrong. It is her faith in this choice which makes the difference.*

Who holds us up? Who leads us? Who heals us?

The *miracle* is that Jesus holds me up. He teaches me to walk on the waters of life by holding His hand, one day at a time.

Tomorrow, next week, next month, next year ... I might need to take medication or to submit to a surgical procedure for breast cancer or for another condition. I'm not against nor afraid of medicine. I only ask that all medical treatment is confirmed by the peace of Jesus reigning in my life.

Anything or anyone violating this peace must be examined very prayerfully. The Holy Spirit is sent to guide me and protect me. *I must not place the wisdom of any man above God's wisdom.*

Ivan and I traveled to the City of Faith to consult

with a surgeon, but looking back we know Jesus arranged another appointment in Tulsa for us.

A young hospital chaplain sat down to talk to us in the doctor's office. We shared our testimony, our situation, and our struggle. He in turn shared these words with us.

"Healing isn't having the right words to confess, or the right Scriptures to repeat. Many people come here and have these and they are not healed.

"Healing isn't having the right medication or the proper surgical procedures or the best medical equipment in the world. Many people come here and have these and they are not healed.

"The majority of people that we see continue on a path of healing are those who search their hearts, consider the risks, the medical options, struggle with God, and find peace. These are the people who are healed.

"It's as if the *peace of God* releases healing within their bodies, both with medical help and without medical help."

The chaplain took us by the hand we joined together in prayer. The peace of God settled in upon us with a mighty anointing. The three of us held hands in silence for several minutes.

He looked up at us after our prayers, shook his head in amazement, and said, "There's no doubt about it. The *peace* of Jesus is with you. Whatever you decide to do, He will be with you. And He will be your Healer."

The Body of Christ has traveled up one road and down another searching for answers to the difficult questions of healing. We've read all the books, heard all the tapes, followed all the teachers.

Still, disappointed Spirit-filled Christians turn away from the ministry of healing, disillusioned and broken, putting up walls, sometimes rejecting God Himself. Have we missed something?

What's the Father saying to His Church today? He calls us to reach for miracles, but why? Is it for the miracles themselves or is it for the work taking place within us as we stretch out our hand of faith and reach out for His? The Father's calling us to a new maturity in Christ and we're learning difficult lessons of faith and trust at the crossroads of life and death.

Once we learn to stand unafraid in the face of our greatest enemy, we're going to walk without fear on the waters of life.

The greatest gift given to me by Ivan, our prayer fellowship, and my surgeon, was the *freedom to choose* without condemnation or pressure to decide on one path over the other. During my confusion, I actually wanted someone to choose for me. But, on the other side of it all, I know their silence was a gift from my Lord.

I believe God wants all of us to learn how to give each other the freedom to choose, to step, and even to sink into the sea of life if necessary, until we reach inside ourselves and grasp the hand of God which is always reaching out for us.

Decisions will continue to press in on us from every side, decisions about health, jobs, where to move, when to move, where to send our children to school, or which church to attend.

We're going to be able to depend less and less on the spiritual stability in other people and the institutions around us. Doctors too often advise treatment, not on the basis of their healing gifts, but on the guidelines of their malpractice insurance.

Governments legalize abortion and take prayer out of our schools.

Churches disregard the Word of God and preach the religion of secular humanism. Or, on the other end of the spectrum, some ministries abuse the Word of God by preaching a gospel of bondage and condemnation in the name of *faith*.

Years ago, men and women relied upon their "gut feelings." In many instances, this remained their chief source of guidance.

Today, man considers himself much too intelligent for such subjective rationale. He studies the facts and statistics. He consults with advisors and makes an objective decision.

Objectivity isn't wrong. We need it. However, when it lacks godly wisdom, it's blind.

Blind objectivity crucified Christ. The same manner of human reasoning is attempting to crucify the Holy Spirit in us by nailing our God-given perceptions of life to a cross of statistics and probability.

The crowds cry out and push us in one direction after another. Public opinion polls make decisions for us before we even ask the question. Men in authority attempt to put down controversy by legislating controls to appease the loud and the arrogant.

Christians who allow themselves to be pushed by the crowds, manipulated by public opinion, and rubber-stamped by legislative dictates soon quench the life of the Holy Spirit. Again and again, God is denied His rightful place as the supreme Authority within us.

The Church must rekindle the guidance ministry of the Holy Spirit. We must get in touch with our life-monitor. Our life depends upon it!

In matters of decision (whether involving health, home, job, family, etc.) we need to test all circumstantial evidence against our inner peace. A gut feeling? Yes!

And when our innermost being is filled with the Holy Spirit, it's a powerful compass to point us in the right direction.

The Scriptures call it "discernment," the ability to distinguish between right and wrong, good and evil. Call it discernment, call it intuition, call it a gut feeling. It doesn't matter *what* we call it — it matters that it's filled with the Spirit of God and that we listen to the Holy Spirit within us.

We can't turn to our Bibles and find the answer to personal questions involving surgery, job changes, schools and ministries.

But the Scriptures do tell us, "Let the peace of Christ rule in your heart" (Col. 3:15).

The *peace of Christ* will always confirm (agree with) a decision based on faith and trust in Jesus Christ. If we don't *trust Him* in a decision, we won't have *peace*, regardless of man's promises.

Trusting our faculties of discernment is like stepping out of a safe boat and attempting to walk on the water. During our season of rest and healing in Florida, Ivan owned a power boat. We enjoyed the Gulf waters and learned a great deal about the unpredictable nature of the sea. We loved to be *in the boat* but lacked all desire to be *in the water.*

Nothing, short of a sinking vessel, could convince me to place my body in the deep water. Strange creatures lurked in there! The brackish harbor water lapped at the sides of the boat, echoing the taunting laughter of the sea. For me, this all remained unknown territory. I preferred the safety and security of the boat.

We all have a spiritual boat — a place to feel safe — a place to keep us floating along on the waters of life. The waves roll in, but as long as our vessel of security remains in good shape, there's not much to worry about.

Sometimes, however, our boat springs a leak and we start to sink. This is the time in our life when we need a miracle — for healing, for financial provision, for the restoration of a relationship, and the list goes on.

We have a choice to make — we can spend the rest of our life bailing water, drown, or get out and walk.

All over the world, Christians need a miracle! In the face of all our needs, we hear the voice of Jesus say, "Come."

In faith and trust, we step out of our boats, defy the odds and keep our eyes on Christ. Then, with each confident step, we witness miracles in our lives and ministries.

Human knowledge and understanding will never produce a Divine miracle. We applaud medical technology for healing miracles and forget who is the Author of life and death.

We bow before computers as they feed us volumes of

information and forget who is the Source of all true knowledge and wisdom.

It is time for God's people to put Him back on the throne of their lives.

God is raising up a people of power — a people who listen wisely to the opinion of man and the full measure of knowledge available. Then, having gleaned man's insight, they humbly submit everything to the *subjection* of their God — the all-knowing One.

He's building a Church without walls to protect His people. He promises to be a wall of fire around us (Zech. 2:1-5). Walls of fear will never protect us or hide us. Rather, they often prevent our escape from the evil one's devices. These walls trap us; they ensnare us; they build a maze of confusion through which we wander aimlessly.

During the coming years we will find ourselves fleeing an onslaught of new age thought and practice. Every corner of our lives will be threatened by its influence, from the education of our minds and the care of our bodies to the foundations of our religious thought and practice.

Wherever we turn, someone will stand ready to make our decisions for us; to ease the responsibility of choice, to absolve us of guilt ... and to promote experimentation and change for the sake of future generations. With each decision someone else makes for us, the walls of dependency and acceptance rise.

Our Father knows these times are upon us. He knows exactly what we need in the face of each crisis, each decision, each dilemma. *He stands ready to give us everything we need to face the crisis, make the decision, and resolve the dilemma — to get out of our boat! He is our All in All!*

This new Church, rising up from the midst of a broken and confused generation, is a miracle-working Church! Not because we have learned how to perform signs and wonders, but because we're finally willing to walk on the water.

Jesus holds out His hand on the waters of life and bids us, "Come."

We look around and see the unstable waves and the unpredictable winds of life. Decisions, decisions, we are multitudes in the valley of decision. However, we're not alone. I wasn't and neither are you.

Our God is here, in the midst of us, building His Church *without the walls of fear and compromise* which keep us from trusting in His supernatural power.

Some say the day of miracles is gone
And they put their trust in man.
God's Word tells me miracles are mine
When I'm led by His Almighty Hand. Jesus says,

"Reach! Reach! Reach for a miracle today!"
Jesus hears us when we pray
So reach for God's miracle,
God's miracle today.

Suggested Scripture Meditation: Matthew 14:27-33
                                    Proverbs 3:5-8

Chapter Five

A Letter of Encouragement to Those Who Will Pass Through Spiritual Seasons

"Be not afraid to grow in My vineyard."

Our bedroom window overlooked Jackie's backyard. Winter snows covered the ground and hid the pathway between our two homes.

Jackie and I shared so much in our walk with Jesus — we were kindred spirits, as some say. I remembered our first song from Jesus with a smile.

"Sing for Me," Jesus continually asked of me.

"What?" I'd reply. "I don't know how to sing. I can't even carry a tune."

"Sing for Me." His call continued to permeate my prayers and refused to leave.

Our small Wednesday night healing service

desperately needed a music ministry — so desperately that Jackie and I pulled out our guitars and learned a few chords together — just enough to carry us over until Jesus sent a "real music ministry."

But "sing" I did not. Jackie sang. I opened and closed my mouth at the appropriate times!

We practiced faithfully and our husbands spent many nights waiting for us to come home from each other's houses via the well-worn path.

One afternoon before our practice an unexpected thought passed through my mind. "Jackie has a song from the Lord. She needs to write it down."

A short time later, at her kitchen table, I blurted out, "You're supposed to write a song."

"A what?"

"A song."

She responded with a blank expression and "I don't know how to write songs. I can't even read music; you know that."

"Well," I tried to explain, "I don't think you need to. The Holy Spirit does it."

I proceeded to tell her the little (the very little) I knew about receiving songs from the Holy Spirit. "Just write down what you hear and the rest will come."

Her expression started to change to a look of recognition. "This must be what's happening. But no, that's impossible..."

"What? Tell me about it!"

"On my way to school every morning, this music keeps going through my head. A few words come with it, and a catchy little tune. It's about creation."

"Write it down. Jesus will give you the rest," I told her excitedly. "You have to accept the little He gives at first to receive more. It's stepping out in faith."

Later that week, back in Jackie's kitchen, we witnessed the completion of "God Created the World" as the last words and portions of music fell together. Her own testimony of receiving the Holy Spirit came to life through the music (see page 45).

The Christmas season arrived, but my mind strayed from manger songs. Every time I practiced my guitar, the story of Peter walking on the water filled my thoughts. Within a short time I held the lyrics to a song in my hand.

"Sing it for me. Let me hear it," Jackie encouraged me.

Well, I tried. I opened my mouth and an awful sound spilled out. I closed it fast and tried again. Jackie didn't say anything, but the strained expression on her face said it all.

It was so frustrating! I could hear the music in my head. I knew the tune and I could feel it. However, try as I might, I could not sing.

"Let's pray," I suggested. "After all, it's about miracles and I really need one now!"

We prayed together in our usual manner — a time of praise, a short request for the help we needed and then a time of waiting for the Holy Spirit to guide us. After our prayer, Jackie quickly reached for her guitar. She struck a couple of chords and started to sing...

My entire body trembled with excitement! She sang the lyrics I had written to the very same tune which ran through my head.

"How did you know?" I asked in dumbfounded amazement.

"I just heard the music in my head. I can't explain it. It's just there and it has to be God, it certainly isn't me."

And on it continued. A hand much more powerful than our own — the hand of God — wove our lives together skillfully and tenderly. In so many ways we moved, thought, and prayed as one to the beat of heaven's songs.

Sisters? Yes — bonded together for reasons we didn't completely understand and in ways which continued to amaze us, from the songs we shared to the time we unknowingly chose identical wallpaper patterns.

Inasmuch as we shared a common joy, we also shared the pain of misunderstandings and separations which plagued our relationship periodically. Our sisterhood in Christ often fell victim to the circumstances of life both within us and around us. My role as the pastor's wife added an extra dimension of complication to our friendship.

Now our guitars gathered dust while the winter snows threatened to completely engulf the small path between our homes. I wanted to run out and kick my way through the snow to open it, defying the forces attempting to separate us. Instead, I turned away from the window with tears spilling from my eyes.

"Why, Lord? Why? You've called us to do so much together for You. You've given us so much together. Why?"

"There's new wine in My Kingdom, daughter."

"What, Lord?"

"New wine. Your fruit remains and it shall be pressed into wine."

New wine ... new life in the Spirit. Joy. Renewal. Now? In this time of winter separation and confusion?

And then, a prophetic word given to Jackie over a year ago flashed through my thoughts. "Beneath the sands of time there lies a vineyard of new wine."

Instinctively, I reached for my guitar. A new song poured from my heart about love in the Kingdom of God. In contrast to the emotion of the previous few minutes, the music danced with joy and excitement.

Over several weeks' time a compilation of Scripture study, prayer, prophetic words, and personal experiences sent this "living letter" into my heart. It is a letter not only to me, but to all of us who struggle with the seasons of change taking place in God's vineyard.

****

My Tender Branch,

Be not afraid to grow in My vineyard. For it is through abiding in Me that you shall bear much fruit, and your fruit shall remain. It will remain as new wine in My Kingdom to be poured out, filling many empty cups which are now lifted up in My Name (John 15:1-7).

Do you remember springtime? That moment when you opened your heart and whispered My Name in faith? Do you remember the love which filled you as My Father gently grafted you into the Vine? You became a part of Me and I a part of you (Rom. 11:17).

Fear not. I want you to understand all of the seasons

A Letter of Encouragement 119

and the process of growth taking place in My Father's vineyard. For in understanding, you will learn the mystery of abiding in Me. This has been a deep desire of your heart for some time. You have lifted many prayers and beseeched My Name for this truth.

First, you must learn to listen for the sounds of spiritual springtime, for the gentle breezes of the Holy Spirit, and for the spring rains (Joel 2:23, Jer. 5:24).

In My Father's vineyard the branches lift their leaves to heaven and sing for the Father to pour out rains of refreshing upon their waiting, thirsty hearts (Psalm 72:6).

Never forget an important truth, My child. You aren't alone. You aren't the only branch grafted into the Vine.

You are surrounded by many other branches which touch your life every day. Their growth, as well as your own, must be carefully considered by the Vinedresser. Far too many branches want to grow alone, independent, untouched by others. This cannot be (1 Cor. 12:12,13,26).

Spring is the time to grow, to put for the new shoots, and to bloom. I rejoice as you grow up and out, stretching forth to reach out in new places, touching one nearby branch and then another, sometimes gently allowing your lives to intertwine.

There are new ways to worship, to pray, to study the written Word, to explore new relationships (Col. 1:9-12).

Understand also that spring always evolves into summer and the time to bear fruit. The warmth of the summer sun stirs you to put forth the fruit which is continually developing within you (Gen. 8:22).

Oh, that you and others will stop striving to bear fruit! This isn't something you can *plan* to do. It's a natural happening because My life is in you and you are in Me. It happens as a result of *abiding* in the Vine (Col. 2:6, John 15:1-7).

There's a fulness of joy in your fellowship with My Father and with each other. There are new calls to ministries producing "fruitful" results. The heat of the summer sun increases and the fruitfulness of your life becomes evident to those around you.

The Father smiles at the productivity in your life. Yet He knows that in a short time, the seasons will change and confusion will fill your heart (Gal. 5:22, Gen. 8:22).

The fruit you bear is in a continual state of change. It is growing, developing, and being harvested. I do not call you to bear plastic fruit, but fruit with *life* which will give life to others. There's much confusion in the vineyard because you do not understand the time of harvest.

The harvest, you see, is also a seasonal happening. It is in the natural order of creation. The Vinedresser comes for His fruit. The fruit belongs to Him and He needs it.

In the natural, the grape harvest is timely. If not picked within a short time, the grapes will lose their sugar content. If left on the vine, the fruit becomes moldy and rotten. Insects and birds devour it and its usefulness to the Vinedresser is ended (Matt. 21:33-41).

My Father carefully tends His vineyard and desires that your fruit *remain* — that it remain in the Kingdom of God. *He will harvest the fruit!*

Love, the sweetest and choicest fruit, if not given away will soon lose its flavor. Love which is held on to and not given to others becomes rotten, infested, and dried up. Eventually it is lost (1 Cor. 13:4).

The Vinedresser knows, as you are now beginning to understand in your own heart, that the fruit you bear is not for yourself — it's for others.

As the hand of the Father reaches for your fruit, He gently whispers, "I need your fruit, daughter. This one over here feels unloved. Love her for Me.

"This servant of mine is depressed. Give him encouragement and joy from your heart.

"This one is anxious ... be patient.

"My Word must be shared over here ... My servants need help over here ... teach, give, share, love...."

Again and again, your fruit is given to the Kingdom of God as you respond to My Father's bidding and His gentle hand as He moves through the vineyard at harvest time.

By the fruit in your life, you are known to all as one who abides in Me. Many, many hungry people reach out as the Father moves through the vineyard (Matt. 7:16).

So many needs, and the need is often greater than you are able to meet.

I've watched you obediently give and give until your tender branches were picked clean. And then, I've watched you fall under the condemnation of the enemy who ridicules your barren branch, calling you unfit for the Kingdom of God (Rom. 8:1).

Only *evil* fruit is condemned, or one who bears *no* fruit! (Matt. 7:19, John 15:2,6)

The Father sees all and He knows that as you abide in the vine, a bountiful harvest of choice, ripe fruit is rising from within you and will come forth in due season.

One who is spent and weary from the demands of ministry must rest and replenish. Even I needed time to rest, to be alone with My Father.

Your spiritual eyes and ears are filled with lies from the accuser. You are unable to hear the song that is ringing through the vineyard.

> *There's new wine in the Kingdom, in the Kingdom of God,*
> *And it's flowing right here for you and me.*
> *Our Father has harvested the fruit from the Vine*
> *And He's lovingly pressed it to wine.*

The Father has harvested your fruit, but it remains! He needs it to produce Kingdom Wine.

"What happens to the fruit?" you ask. "Where does it go?"

Long ago, when God's people celebrated the harvest, they used the fruit for several purposes. Some was eaten fresh, providing nourishment and enjoyment for the moment.

Much of your fruit is like that. You give love, joy, peace and patience for an immediate need and the Father is pleased. In obedience, you produce fruitful works of helps and ministry for those in need. Although this fruit is in a constant state of growth and development within you, it is given to others at specific moments in time.

Some grapes were dried for raisins and stored for a

later use. Remember the time you were gifted with a word of encouragement and hope? Weeks, perhaps months later, My Spirit rekindled that very word of encouragement to you at a time when you needed it. Memories such as this, stored away for later use, are My Father's little "raisins."

The majority of the grapes, however, were tossed into the winevats or presses. By crushing the fruit, it was transformed into a substance which could be *poured out* for many.

I know, My child, that it's painful for you to watch the fruit of your ministry crushed until it's not recognizable to you. I know the confusion which fills your heart as the love you so freely yielded to the Father is squeezed until only the empty hulls remain. Confusing, yes; but all a part of the Father's plan.

The people of Israel celebrated during the time of harvest. They danced and sang because they knew the finished product would be...

> Poured out on the altars as a sacrificial gift (Lev. 23:13).
> Used for its healing properties (1 Tim. 5:23, Luke 10:34).
> Used as a tithe (Deut. 14:22-23).
> Used as food and refreshment (John 2:1-9).

Yes, as with all of God's gifts, it was often used and abused for man's sinful purposes.

Arise! Stand tall. Cast off the spirit of confusion and the accusations of the evil one! There is no condemnation. Accept the seasons of change and growth in the vineyard! Your fruit remains!

Every word, every deed, every song, every prayer, every kind thought given in Jesus' Name *remains* and will be poured out for the Body of Christ!

As the harvest ends it is time to lift your barren branches for the Father's pruning knife. Yes, this must be so, that you might bear more fruit, abundant fruit, everlasting fruit.

It is during this season that many turn away, unable to trust in My Father's all-knowing love and wisdom. The blade of the Vinedresser's knife comes swiftly, cutting away long graceful branches and new growth.

Does this sound harsh? Oh, but it is harsher still to allow the vineyard to grow wild and untended, producing bitter fruit (Is. 5:1-10).

The Father prunes with unbounded love, for He knows the dangers of uncontrolled spiritual growth. He sees that which you are not able to see and protects you from many spiritual pitfalls and snares.

I know you're filled with doubt and misunderstanding. Something wonderful has been taken away from you. The abundance which filled your life is gone.

Oh, my daughter, it is so easy to grow long stretching shoots in the wrong direction. These shoots become filled with pride and choke out the younger and smaller branches trying to grow beside you.

Remember, you are not alone on the vine. There are times you must be painfully pruned to protect others' growth. There is no room for selfish growth in the Father's vineyard.

Pruning time passes and your repentant heart releases the healing sap from the Vine. As you cry out

A Letter of Encouragement 125

to Me, My life pours forth healing virtues to help you change and grow in ways which will be pleasing to the Father.

Winter arrives in the vineyard. It is time to rest, to reflect. The summer sun no longer stirs you to growth and even the sound of the Father's footsteps and the voice of His singing is silenced. Your branches no longer reach out and touch one another. You are together on the vine, yet alone.

During this season you will learn the secret of abiding in Me. Yes, the cold winds will come and the snows will cover the ground.

But you shall sense a new inner strength pouring forth from deep within. For you are in Me and I in you. You will not pass through the winter alone. I am here, as always. Together we will share the secrets of silence.

This is a time the Father has set aside for us. *Do not be afraid to enter into it.* Spend time with Me and in My Word. Reflect upon the seasons which have passed and the Vinedresser's work in your life.

Spring will come again and the gentle rains will give you fresh expectations. The summer sun will stir you to new growth and you will bear abundant fruit for Kingdom Wine.

The harvest will always remind you that your life belongs to the Father. Pruning time will always be painful. However, as you mature, there will be less and less wild growth to cut away.

Winters will be a time of separation — dying to the past and preparing for the future. They will be long or short, dependent upon your willingness to allow My

Spirit to accomplish His work within you. It is all dependent upon your will.

Earthly seasons are bound by the laws of creation. Spiritual seasons are not. One individual may take years to pass through a single cycle of growth. Another may pass through these changes in a few hours.

I am the Vine and you are the Branches. We shall grow as one in the Kingdom of God. Your life is mine and mine is yours. Do not be afraid of the growth which is calling you to pass through the seasons. For without the seasons, there will be no wine.

In season and out,
I will always remain,
The True and Everlasting Vine

Brothers and sisters, the branches are we,
And the Vine is our Lord Jesus Christ,
The fruit of our lives will be changed into wine
And given for others, you see...

Oh, come, Holy Spirit, and pour out Your love
All sent from the Father above,
But given to us through the lives of our friends
Friends who abide in Your love.

For there's new wine in the Kingdom, in the Kingdom of God
And it's flowing right here for you and me,
Our Father has harvested the fruit from the vine
And lovingly pressed it to wine.

Suggested Scripture Meditation: John 15

Chapter Six

A Letter of Decision to Those Who Are Called to Choose

"Be not afraid of new wineskins."

There's no place to hide anymore. Nor are we able to pretend that the dilemma of the wineskin doesn't exist.

From the valleys to the mountaintops, across the rivers and into the deserts, the Spirit of God continues to lead an exodus of believers away from mainline denominations.

The emphatic marching orders sometimes take many of us by surprise. Sadly, we find ourselves unequipped and ill prepared for the journey ahead of us.

Still, driven by an uncompromising desire to follow

our Lord, we join the untold thousands of Charismatic Christians who have evacuated their churches in an effort to save themselves and their children from an onslaught of religious persecution.

This persecution appears to follow every step of obedience, every word of witness, every pledge of heartfelt allegiance to the Lord Jesus Christ.

It disguises itself behind religious traditions, but the end result is always the same: Born-again Charismatic Christians are often identified as unwelcome guests in their own churches. *The walls of misunderstanding* go up and do not come down.

Many of us feel the pressure of a mighty door closing behind us, pushing us out into exile.

We want to stop it from closing, from locking us out. Yet the door continues to close. Eventually we're forced out into a strange new world of spiritual accountability.

The cities change. The denominations change. The names and faces change. The circumstances change from place to place, but the basic story remains the same.

The old wineskin (the church structure) cannot accommodate the new wine (fresh spiritual experiences). There's not enough room for expression, for growth, for understanding, or for the disciplined life of holiness required by the Holy Spirit. The old against the new — an ageless battle refusing to cease.

Ivan and I never considered ourselves "comer-outers" (those who hear the call to separate from religious institutions and seek refuge in independent or Pentecostal ministries). If anything, we openly discouraged it.

We held fast to the conviction that Spirit-filled believers should work within their home congregations for spiritual renewal. This belief formed the foundation of our renewal ministry within our denomination. Stay and pray! Witness and work! Love and be loved! All in the Name of Jesus our Lord!

We believed in the historical roots of our denomination and we prayed continually for the restoration of our spiritual heritage. We wrestled with doctrine and tradition as we attempted to find our place in a maze of theological dogmas which allowed little room for experiential Christianity.

Finally, through the pages of historical writings we identified with the spiritual fathers of our denomination. We started to understand our spiritual journey from their perspective.

These men of God believed in a personal conversion experience, the empowering presence of the Holy Spirit and the manifestation of spiritual gifts. They lived in the Word of God, prayer, and holiness (as did the majority of our church fathers, regardless of denomination).

Understanding our denominational heritage from this perspective held us fast, but we refused to allow the religious traditions of men to hold us back — to keep us from following the Word of God and the voice of His Holy Spirit.

This refusal to bow down to traditions, coupled with an adventurous desire to explore new frontiers in our own spirituality, placed us in opposition to the vast majority within our denomination and also to a segment of our own congregation.

And this is the place that I know many of you still find yourselves today — torn between an unquenchable hunger for the things of God and a congregation or denomination that insists, "Be content with the portion you have received. It's been enough for us. It will be enough for you."

Some Christians choose to live in yesterday's move of God, never feeling a need or a desire to experience anything more.

Others find satisfaction as their tradition is enhanced with a fresh perspective and subtle changes in worship.

Still others seek after God with all their heart and allow Him to radically change their lives. This transforming work of the Holy Spirit is often likened to new wine, fermenting within the wineskin. The new wine needs room to breathe and expand (to work) in order to produce a life of Kingdom Wine.

It is quite impossible for mainline denominational Christians to be involved in spiritual renewal and not be touched in some fashion by the wineskin dilemma. You have either found satisfaction in the "old" and preferred to remain in traditional religion, or your thirst for the "new" has set you in opposition to the church of your youth.

Family and friends are now expressing their spirituality in both respects and the common understanding we once shared is only a memory.

We are one in Christ Jesus, but not always one in our experience of His love.

We don't use the same words.

We pray in different ways.

We have a variety of expectations for the Christian

life. I've walked too many roads to presume that I know the perfect way. I'm called to remain faithful to the understanding which I have at the present time and to walk in this revelation of His love. You must do the same.

Sometimes, as I learned in the valley of inner healing, love is letting go. And, as I needed to learn again, letting go isn't always easy.

Making a choice isn't always easy. Yet, the truth of the wineskin calls us to choose.

****

"It's over, Jean. Let it go. It's time to move on," my husband insisted with firm conviction rising in his voice.

"Isn't there some way; isn't there something we can do? This is our home. This congregation is our family. How can we leave?"

"That's not the question, Jean. The question is, *'How can we possibly stay?'* I'm not certain how long our family is going to be safe here — there's too much happening, in the physical realm as well as the spiritual. God is telling us to go and to go now!"

My husband spoke the truth, regardless of the fact that I refused to receive it as such.

Why, Lord?

Just a short time ago we sang songs of love and rejoiced together as the Holy Spirit moved among us. Finally, after all those years, we enjoyed a season of fulfillment. Attendance and membership increased. Sunday morning stirred with anticipation as we introduced choruses of praise and worship, blending them with the familiar liturgical responses. Adult Sunday School classes increased, mid-week study groups thrived, and we praised the Father for His faithfulness.

The finances of the congregation also experienced the bounty of God, with an abundance to give to Church-wide organizations and missionary efforts. Then, in an overwhelming expression of their love, the congregation completely renovated the parsonage for us.

Ivan taught the Word of God with a renewed sense of expectation and purpose. Ears previously deaf to biblical understanding suddenly opened and willingly accepted the call to discipleship.

The battleground of yesterday remained only a memory. Restored and healed, we embraced each other with new insight and an increased love. Our relationships had faced the test of forgiveness and now stood strong against the spirits of pride, jealousy, and debate.

A circle of prayer warriors formed and the Holy Spirit knit us together with tight bonds of love and friendship. We started to experience the true meaning of community.

True, not everyone in the congregation participated — but patiently we watched the circle grow wider one by one. Nearly one third of our congregation had experienced the Baptism of the Holy Spirit or made a life-changing commitment to Jesus Christ.

We continued to pray for the renewal of the whole church. Blessed and secure, Ivan and I settled in for many long years of fruitful ministry.

But one Sunday morning, a series of circumstances began to unfold. One misunderstanding led to another and soon it appeared as though the entire scenario were engineered and planned by the prince of darkness himself.

I stood at the very center of the controversy. Ivan and I tried to clarify the situation, but every effort to stand on truth backfired into a thunderous barrage of misinterpretations and falsehoods.

Overnight, members turned against us, refusing to accept our leadership and ministry as we stood behind a decision made by our Church Council to implement a constitutional provision for church discipline.

Others stood with us — the council leadership, the prayer warriors, pastoral friends and counselors. Slowly, one by one we watched their lives face the same misunderstanding and rejection by those who considered the disciplinary action unjustified.

Ugly rumors turned into bold lies and the lies into threats against our ministry. My husband held me in his arms. We both shook with the emotion of knowing that our ministry could never be the same again — not in this place.

"If we ignore this," Ivan reminded me, "we stand guilty with the prophets who cried, ' "Peace, peace," when there is no peace' (Jer. 6:14).

"The problem isn't ours, Jean. It didn't begin with us and won't end with us. Quite honestly, I don't believe it will ever be resolved with us here."

Yes, the root problem of resistance to change and to all who dared to institute change had manifested itself through the years to former pastors, their families, and even congregational members. But never before had the problem become so explosive, nor had anyone dared confront it openly.

I wanted to believe that we were different, that our ministry here could offer effective spiritual renewal.

I cried, I pleaded. I begged my husband to change his mind.

"It's over, Jean. We're going to leave and you need to face this fact. That is, of course, unless you want to stay here without me!" he told me with a cold, determined look in his eyes.

His heart had already left. Packing and moving was only a formality.

I wanted to go on, to compromise if I must, but to keep the life I knew and loved. I wanted Jesus to take this nightmare away.

For three days and nights I did not sleep. Wide-eyed, I sat in our darkened livingroom, heart-wrenching sobs spilling forth from deep within.

Personal rejection is one thing. But the rejection of my husband's ministry and of our lives poured out for the sake of the Gospel cut deeply and without mercy.

Jesus within us, rejected by those He loved so very much ... I just didn't have enough resources within me to cope with the depth of my feelings.

My husband moved through the routine of ministry, but his joy had disappeared. Every day he fought against a violent surge of emotion, wanting to strike back.

Looking me straight in the eye he confessed in desperation, "Jean, I've got to get out of here before I do or say something I'll regret for the rest of my life."

"Isn't there something we can do? Don't you want to see this through ... to stand for what you believe?"

"It doesn't matter what I want — or even what I believe. I don't have the strength to go on. I'm tired of fighting this endless battle. It just keeps reappearing with a different set of circumstances. *It's a wall that will not come down.*

"Besides, Jean, I'm worried about you. You know what the doctors have warned us about the effect of stress and the recurrence of cancer. I'm just not ready to consign my life, your life, or the kids' lives to go on this way."

He picked up the mail from our kitchen counter and leafed through it. An item from our denomination's office fell out of his hands and back onto the counter. Without a word, Ivan headed for his office.

I stared at the rejected envelope and remembered the phone call Ivan had made to the denominational office. He asked for help, expecting his brothers in Christ to stand with him, to help, and to advise. For the sake of the congregation, he wanted to take everything through the proper channels.

Instead of prayerful support and advice, they answered emphatically, "This is a congregational problem and we won't get involved."

Thus, we turned to our pastoral friends in renewal and asked them to pray for us. The counsel we received was clear — "Go ... and go now."

And on our knees in prayer, the silence of God encircled us with an ever-present sense of impending danger.

I wanted to recreate the past few days, to do things

A Letter of Decision 137

differently, to say things differently. I hated the events which had transpired, yet I knew they had to take place just as surely as Judas had to betray Jesus. Betrayed, our ministry was placed on trial by telephone gossip lines and crucified by the shouting crowds.

But praise God! Death always gives way to new life. His resurrection power always calls us forth from our tombs of darkness and despair!

One morning as I finished making our bed, the voice of Jesus interrupted my thoughts. *"It's time to go, Jean. Will you come with Me?"*

I looked around my lovely home and whispered, "I don't belong here anymore, do I Lord?"

I smoothed the bedspread corners and wiped away the tears spilling from my eyes. I wanted to stay so badly. Once again I faced the test of obedience.

Jesus had sent us here for a purpose eight years ago — to reach and teach as many as would listen. Many listened and received. Jesus reigned in their hearts and their lives. They listened to His voice in the silent places and sang a song of praise to their God.

Regardless of the circumstances surrounding us, the season for our ministry in this place had now moved to a close. Biting my lip, I submitted to the will of God. "Yes, Lord, I'll come."

The next few days I turned my attention to moving. Ivan was already busy making plans for an investigative trip to southwest Florida. He made his travel plans enthusiastically, without any hint of regret.

Moving means packing. Packing means sifting and sorting. What shall I keep? What shall I toss? I pulled out the drawer of my filing cabinet and rubbed my hands thoughtfully over the cluttered files.

"I never did manage to organize these," I muttered, reprimanding myself as I sat down to wade through the sea of papers and file folders. Time slipped away while I read through notes and lesson plans for Sunday School classes, Mother's Discussion Group, and Bible studies.

Some flipped into the wastebasket without any sense of remorse. Others, reminding me of those special times when God's Spirit moved in with a rich anointing, found their way into a neat pile of "things to keep."

Midway through the drawer I pulled out the folder with "Prophecies" scribbled across the front. Since the early days of the prayer ministry, the Lord had asked us to write down and keep all visions, prophecies and words from Him.

We did this for several reasons...

to confirm one another,

to learn from our mistakes,

to see God's Word come to pass over a period of time,

to attempt to understand His Word to us as individuals and a fellowship,

and, if for no other reason, as an act of obedience because Jesus asked us to.

I read through all His beautiful promises and choked back a rush of emotion. "Why, Lord?"

We saw praising people with hands lifted to heaven. We saw miracles and healings. We saw maps with indications that our ministry in this place would reach to a large area and even out across the country. Visiting evangelists prophesied renewal and a wide outreach from our congregation. Much had come to pass, but there was so much more ... so much yet to be accomplished. Why didn't we see it?

There, hidden in between the promises, lay some of the earlier prophecies that Cappy and I had received as we first prayed for the birth of the prayer ministry. I read them closely.

Shrouded in scriptural symbolism, these visions were filled with warnings of impending conflict ... snakes hidden under rocks, fires, floods, dying plants, and unmovable structures made by man.

"Oh, Lord Jesus! Why didn't we see? Why didn't we rise up in intercessory prayer against this evil? Why were we so slow to understand?"

At the back of the file I pulled out some photocopies of a statement I'd found several months ago in some very old church records. The history of God's people always intrigued me, and here from a ledger page dated 1873, in the stately penmanship of that era, these words shouted at me:

> No so-called "new measures," "anxious bench systems," or the like, in doctrine or in practice, shall ever be tolerated in any shape or form in this congregation.

My thoughts drifted back to the time I first found this old constitution. I'd researched "New Measures" and learned that "New Measures" referred to all changes resisted by the established church of the day. The clothing ministers wore, the use of hymn books and musical instruments in church, kneeling in prayer, women's prayer meetings ... these and so many more were described as "New Measures." The "Anxious

Bench System" was an altar call, or praying with any form of emotion at the altar.

When I first read those words of that old constitution, they interested me. But now, in the midst of all this, these same words jumped off the page with revelation and life. *This proclamation still lived among us!*

Lord? Could it be? Is there a link between the spiritual heritage of this congregation and what's happening to us today?

I considered the resistance we had encountered during the years of our ministry. Every change, large or small, always sparked dissention among us.

The prayer ministry and the ministries to which it gave birth resulted in a continual cry for change and growth. Although this pleased us, Ivan spent a major part of his ministry putting out fires of protest that cried, "This is the way it's always been here, and we don't want to change."

In many respects, Ivan stood as the pastoral shepherd of two distinct congregations. While one clung to the traditions of the past — both religious and social — the other cried for change, for renewal, and for the congregation to forge ahead into the Promised Land. Constantly torn between two ministries (both of which he loved in different ways), he was tired and burned out.

It all started to make sense. From a time long ago, in the history of our congregation, the words of our forefathers had destined the congregation to a life of tradition and resistance to change.

"So for the sake of your tradition, you have made void the Word of God" (Matt. 15:6).

Proud and unwavering, the voices of these men echoed down through the generations with the stern disciplines of their age, and now a curse of spiritual bondage to our generation.

I believe a curse can be broken in the Name of Jesus. I wanted to storm the gates of heaven in prayer and demand that these chains of historical bondage fall to the ground. I wanted to ... but the Spirit of God stopped me.

"This isn't your battle. It belongs to those who sit in leadership. The choice is theirs and must remain with them. They alone have the authority to revoke this spiritual mandate."

I wanted to run to these men and women — they loved us and wanted us to stay. After all, maybe something could still be changed. Again, God stopped me.

"No, this is not your battle, Jean."

"But, Lord?"

"Remember the wineskin?"

"The wineskin, Lord?"

"Be not afraid, for I am calling you forth and will place you in a new wineskin, one ready to accept the changes taking place within your lives. One with room to grow and a freedom in ministry you have not known before.

"The day of My coming is near and there is much to be accomplished. The fields are white unto harvest. My people don't have untold numbers of years to debate the form of worship, the interpretation of My Word, the ownership of a building. The time for debate has passed.

"My Word comes forth in this hour to *prepare* for My coming and I am giving you new wineskins, places of safety and refuge, places with room to grow in My Word, places where the fruit of your lives will be poured out to a thirsty people."

"But, Lord ... You promised us so much in this place. We believed the visions and the prophecies. You promised us a church filled with people who want to praise You, people who will receive healing and miracles; people who will have an impact all over the country. Why didn't it happen, Jesus; why?"

"My Word will accomplish the work I have sent it forth to accomplish. It will not return void. You have received prophetic promises which have given you eyes to see the Church I am raising up in the midst of My people, a church without the walls of debate. You shall see every promise fulfilled as you go forth to minister in My Name. Be not afraid of this work, daughter; be not afraid."

****

Yet the truth is, we are afraid. We don't want to pay the price. We don't want to choose. We don't want to separate from those we love, those we've grown up with. It feels unloving, unjust, even unscriptural.

We're ingrained with the conviction to "stay and pray until death do us part."

The Mother Church whom we loved and upon whom we depended, who nurtured us through many difficult times, is often forced to push us from her womb just as surely as a mother's body forces a baby out into the world during the birth experience.

Each resistance to change may be likened to a labor pain. Circumstances sometimes change and the pain subsides, but it will always return, harder and more insistent, demanding an ultimate separation.

The birth may be well-planned, surrounded by many prayers and a great deal of love. Or it may be unexpected, filled with the pain and violence of human misunderstandings.

The mother stands neither guilty nor innocent before God. It's a fact of life. There's a time to be born. For some of us, as it was for Ivan and me, it is time to leave the womb.

For others, that time has not arrived and the Father will continue to keep them cradled in the womb of Mother Church. Many pastors and congregational members alike will continue to hear the call to minister renewal within the denominations and they will continue to receive the power to walk in obedience.

This is neither right nor wrong. It's the Father's heart alone which decides for each one of us. He alone knows the mysterious birthing process which must take place as He raises His Church to new life.

He alone knows the walls which must come down and when they must fall. He will tear down the walls, but He will not destroy us in the process. The Father loves His Church!

He alone must carefully watch over the formation of each room, filling these rooms with the breath of His life and linking them together with a unity of spirit and understanding unparalleled in historical denominations.

Although His Spirit reigns in majesty among many

large Spirit-filled churches, a great majority of Christians are returning to the catacombs. They're banding together in secret places for prayer and worship. Everywhere His people meet, in large numbers or small, *He builds His Church without walls* and the gates of hell shall not prevail against it.

Each room, like each child born into this work, is unique, designed by the Spirit of God and destined to fulfill the Creator's plan. Even now these rooms are opening their doors to receive the weary pilgrims who have traveled many miles in search of a place to rest. But where are these rooms?

Too often we expect to find our place of refuge in a church building. Sometimes we do, but Jesus isn't interested in the doors of great cathedrals and worship centers. It is the door of our hearts which must open before all other doors.

The door of His *Church without walls* is a humble door, marked by the blood of the Lamb and opened by those who *hear His voice*. As Jesus enters in to sup with us, we enter into a new dimension of His living presence.

His Spirit causes us to yearn for unity — to be able to dwell with one another in Spirit and in Truth.

A place where His voice is heard above all other voices.

A place where obedience is counted all joy.

A place of healing.

A place where the war games are no longer played.

A place for the fruit of our lives to be transformed into Kingdom Wine.

And a place to prepare for the coming of the King of Kings and Lord of Lords.

Ivan and I know the wineskin story well, and we have learned to accept its truth. We left the security of the wineskin we knew and loved. It was a wineskin conformed to the spiritual life it had held for many years — no longer pliable or easily stretched by the process of change. Although we loved it, God called us to a new ministry.

Our decision pushed us from the womb of Mother Church and all the security we enjoyed within her. We embarked on a pilgrimage in search of the new Church rising up in our hearts, a Church without walls.

This pilgrimage led our family to churches and fellowships in Florida and then back to our homeland. New denominations, new styles of worship, large congregations, small fellowships — we're willing to experience them all in our search for a place to bow our heads in prayer and lift our hands in worship.

"Where do we belong, Jesus?"

There is always a part in each of us that wants to go home; I am no exception. But I looked back and realized that "home" no longer existed — at least not the one I remembered.

Jesus reminded me, "No one who puts his hand to the plow and looks back is fit for the Kingdom of God."

"Forgive me, Jesus."

There is only one way to go — forward into the desert, placing the memories of yesterday beneath my feet and following the rainbow of promise in my heart.

We, like so many other Christians searching for a new place to call our spiritual home, traveled from one oasis to another, diligently praying for a place to settle down, to grow in and to call "home."

Many wonderful Spirit-filled Christians in Florida offered us a place to rest under the shade (covering) of their fellowships. We're thankful for their love and their prayers. We're thankful for the Living Water of the Holy Spirit flowing in their midst.

Yet, compelled by the Spirit of God to continue our journey, we needed to press on through the desert. A prophetic word burned in our spirits and prepared us to embark on a new season in God. *"A new Church I'm building, a house without walls."*

Some of us will continue to press on. Some will stay. But all of us will face the fears of separation embedded in our hearts and the undying truth of the wineskin.

Suggested Scripture Meditation: Matthew 9:17

Chapter Seven

A Letter of Confirmation to Those Who Experience the Miracle of Birth

"Be not afraid of the rebirth of My Church."

The cycle of life in ministries must continue — birth and rebirth. People give birth to people, continually replenishing these ministries because our time on this earth is limited by our humanity.

Old forms eventually give way to new. Each generation, by nature of its spiritual giftings, infuses the Church with new life and participates in the rebirth of the whole Body.

Still, a span of time remains where both must coexist — the old and the new. And coexistence often means that ministries must physically separate from one another to survive, the old wine parting from the new so that both may be preserved.

I see the practical implications of this, but my heart

still cries out for more *understanding.* Someplace deep inside my spirit, I sense an incompleteness because I don't *understand* why the rebirth of the Church we love must involve so much pain and confusion for so many people.

I had prayed in so many ways and on so many different occasions since we experienced separation from our congregation. I could see and understand the truth of the wineskin principle from God's Word. I watched this truth live in our lives and the lives of countless others in renewal.

"But in spite of this, Lord, I don't believe You've led us and hundreds of thousands of other Christians into Charismatic Renewal to sadly remind us at the end, 'It's the story of the wineskin. You just can't put new wine in the old wineskin.'

"I need to understand more! I believe You're a God who finishes the work He sets out to do!

"Please! Help me to understand. Help me to silence the questions within!"

I'm not the only one on my knees. Many of you pray for this understanding also — in many ways. Some of you find yourselves participating in intercessory prayer as never before.

The Holy Spirit is compelling you to pray at unusual hours and in unusual ways.

You are crying out with loud cries in the Name of Jesus!

You are weeping at the foot of the cross.

Some of you, having emptied yourselves, are standing in silence before a Holy God — waiting for Him to guide the next whisper from your heart.

We cry out for understanding until our very prayers prepare our hearts to receive His truth. I know I am often slow to understand and deaf to His voice because I'm neither prepared nor willing to hear. It is as though His truth begins to rise up from deep within me (where His Holy Spirit dwells) and it is hindered, stuffed down, overridden, or simply rejected by my conscious mind in self-justification.

My Heavenly Father is never slow to speak to me, nor to help me to understand. I am, however, often very slow to receive that which He imparts to me. Thus, He waits patiently until I'm willing to listen to His voice with an open heart.

I didn't set out to write about the separations taking place in ministries today. That's a topic, I had decided, better left to men and women much wiser than I. Yet the Holy Spirit stopped me and sent me to my knees. When I rose up, I faced a truth I didn't want to face. I accepted a truth which conflicted with many of the decisions Ivan and I have made.

I acknowledged the truth of my Heavenly Father's plan for all of life over the rationale and popular opinion of man and many religious institutions.

And as always, accepting His truth set me free!

The following letter doesn't hold all the answers I'm searching for — but it is a beginning, a place to start looking at where we've come from during the years of Charismatic Renewal and where we are going to allow God to take us in the future.

Again, please remember — this is a compilation of prayers, of the voice of Jesus as I heard it in prayer and through circumstances, of Scripture study and life experiences. This is the voice of the Father speaking to me *through my entire life in Him,* not a word-by-word prophecy. Please receive it prayerfully and allow the Father to impart understanding for your life and ministry.

****

Dear Daughter,

I am a God of order and all of creation follows My plan — life gives life. Physical life gives physical life. Spiritual life is born only of My Spirit. Life begets life. My Church is no exception. My Church is a living organism and must reproduce life. Behold, My Church is pregnant with new life, and the travail of labor has begun.

It is not, nor ever has been, ordained by My Word for ministries to swell with new life until they burst like old wineskins filled with new wine. The wine is spilled. The people are scattered and the new breath of life is snuffed out before it begins.

It is not My desire for ministries to birth new life and then reject it, saying, "You're different ... you must belong to someone else." Rejected, these weak Believers must search for loving fellowships to take them in and love them as their own. Many are adopted. Still others, rejected by the congregations of their birth, are wandering aimlessly in search of love and acceptance.

Still again, I'm not a murderer and I am standing in judgment over ministries who are aborting the young at the first sign of spiritual awakening. My Son is received as Savior and Lord. Lives are opened and filled with My Holy Spirit. Then these young lives are cruelly subjected to the sharp knife of criticism and their spirituality is dissected like a cancerous tumor.

Yes, daughter, all of this and more is taking place even now during the rebirth of My Church. *This is not from My hand; do not attempt to understand it as from My hand!*

I have loved and will continue to love My Church of past generations, but My heart rejoices for the babe coming forth in this hour because this babe — this new generation of My Church — will prepare to meet My Son in His soon return.

Oh, that My people — My Church — will cooperate in this birthing process! Oh, that My Church will rejoice in the new life which now springs forth!

The appointed hour of birth does not come upon you unaware. You've felt the signs of new life and the gentle movements within your midst. The slow but definite growth has stretched the boundaries of traditional ministry. You know what's happening just as surely as a woman with child acknowledges the changes taking place in her body.

It is essential to make preparation for the day of birth! For then, the wineskin will no longer burst. Rather, it shall be *transformed into the womb of life*, as My Church is reborn in your midst.

I will endue My people with a power not known before. The borders of this Church will encompass those who have loved her like the child who grows to tenderly love and care for the aged parent.

The choice is yours, My daughter, and all who have ears to hear. The hour of birth is at hand. It will be as you have prepared for it — a time of great joy or a time of great pain and travail. Regardless, My Church shall be reborn in the midst of My people and will shine forth in the likeness of My Son as never before.

The structures are falling away. The walls are coming down. My Church lives and breathes with the life of My Spirit!

Congregations with ears to hear will give birth to congregations, ministries to ministries, and fellowships to fellowships.

Those who walk in obedience to My Spirit will no longer die in childbirth because they refuse to give birth at the appointed time, and their wombs of life will no longer erupt like the wineskin.

Pastors with ears to hear will lovingly assume the role of helping new ministries to grow from parent ministries instead of building evangelical empires. Their congregations will no longer face division, but they will be filled with the joy of multiplication as they encourage the birth of new ministries.

A unity in My Spirit shall transcend the walls of physical boundaries, membership rolls, and denominational dominion. The mind of man will rend his garments and cry, "This is not the way for a church to grow!" But the mind stayed on Christ will rejoice in the multiplication of ministry gifts, the open doors of ministry, and a Church without walls.

The answers for which you have longed have been as close to you as life itself. I am the same, yesterday, today, and tomorrow. I have created life to give life.

I am and remain,
The Father of All Life

Oh, Father, forgive me. I see now as I've never seen before. We felt those movements of new life within our congregation. Ivan and I knew ... yes, a new church existed within our midst. So many of us knew.

We felt guilty — as if it shouldn't have happened. We thought we were supposed to be one church — not two. We tried to stop it from happening. But we kept praying for new life and You kept sending it.

Some received and walked in newness of life. They received the fulness of Your Spirit, waited in Your presence, praised Your Name in new ways and listened to Your voice. The walls of tradition fell down. Others remained content in the ministry of past generations.

Our human understanding compelled us to keep the congregation together at all costs. This is the mandate of the institution and we pledged our allegiance to it. We dared not defy it.

Oh yes, Father, we felt the gentle nudge of your Holy Spirit, urging us to accept this new church growing within our midst and to nurture it like a child in the womb ... even to accept the eventual separation. But it all seemed so wrong, so against everything we'd been taught about church renewal.

Oh, forgive us, Father, for submitting to the voice of human reasoning.

Then, the travail of birth. The hard, consuming contractions, one body pushing against another. We tried to explain them away, discipline them away, pray them away; but the pain persisted.

The greater our resistance, the greater the misunderstanding and confusion. Forgive us, Father, for defying Your greatest miracle — the miracle of birth. Forgive us for the pain we've inflicted upon one another.

Ivan and I ran as far away as we could to avoid the birthing process — as if our absence might afford a Divine delay of events and prevent an ultimate separation in the congregation.

You released us. You watched us run. You watched us reject this new church, just a babe, crying out for life and guidance.

You watched us reject the church of past generations, stretched to its limits by the demands of ministry. The gifted new life in her midst felt more like a tremendous burden than a blessing — like a mother weighted down with her unborn child, anxious to deliver, eager to be free from the heavy, sometimes painful, burden she carries.

And then you watched us mourn for the ministry we left behind. Yes, because we knew. Deep down in our hearts, we knew the truth. Our conscious minds justified our actions, but our hearts wept. Forgive us, Father.

Distance. Time. We started to understand.

You reunited us for a short visit with so many of those who were crying out for direction. They spoke of a soon-coming decision. They questioned how much longer they'd be welcome in the congregation. They cried in pain. They prayed with hope. And we felt at one with them once again.

Why the cruel turn of events, Lord? Why was our love and concern for one another misunderstood and used as an instrument to attempt the abortion of this new church? I know that You have told me it is not by Your hand that such things take place. But it's so hard to forgive. Help us, Father, to forgive that which we cannot possibly understand.

Restricted by our denominational authorities and separated by physical miles, we stood helpless against the unsuccessful abortion, yet violent birth of this new church. We wept for the child. We wept for the mother. And we struggled with deep emotion against those who raised their hands against them both.

And the babe? A fledging fellowship of believers, rejected by the congregation of its birth, wept in secret places until one by one You led them to places of safety and refuge.

Today, we watch them grow in Your love, from a distance, with the heart of parents who have signed their children away for adoption. Forgive us, Lord.

And everywhere You lead us, we continue to see the signs of new life stirring within ministries. We can't escape the drama of life within Your Church.

Will the wineskin burst again?

Will still another congregation nearly die in childbirth?

Or will Your voice be heard above all other voices as the walls of resistance come down and Your people cry out for guidance in this hour?

As You spoke through the voice of the angel to the mother of our Lord Jesus Christ, speak to Your people and remind us again; "Be not afraid."

Suggested Scripture Meditation: Isaiah 66:8b-10

Chapter Eight

A Letter of Anticipation to Those Who Wait for the Bridegroom's Return

"Be not afraid to prepare for My return!"

Sometimes my faith is stretched to the limit. It feels as though I'm asked to endure hardships far beyond my strength and even my ability to trust in God for His strength.

Like the children of Israel, I find myself tempted to cry out, "Send me back to Egypt, where life was so simple!"

We're not always delighted with the path in front of us...
whether a walk on the waters of faith,
a march through the battlefields,
a slow pace through the valley,
or a trek up the mountain — it's a difficult walk!

God often pushes us to extremes. He exerts pressures from every side. There's little time to simply bask in the glory of God by the beaten path. We're compelled by the Spirit to keep moving!

The mind of man ignores our quest with a toss of his head. This path of discipleship is hardly worth his attention in a world filled with monetary concerns on one hand and pleasure-filled eccentricities on the other. Who has time to indulge in such religious disciplines?

However, every Christian submitted to the Lordship of Christ in this hour knows he must *make time* at all costs. Why? Because Jesus Christ is coming back and *we must be ready!*

The Father's not sending the Body of Christ through this rigorous school of the Spirit for naught. *Everything He does has been and always will be for a Divine purpose.* He's preparing His people for the final harvest.

It's time to stop gazing at our own religious territory and catch the Father's vision for His Church. We're not alone in this school of faith. Every day the lessons are repeated over and over again for individuals, for fellowships, and for congregations.

It's not for our sake that this great drama in time unfolds. As always, it is for His Name's sake, for His glory and for His soon return!

Thus, I share *my understanding* of His coming with you. I'm praying for you to draw nigh unto Jesus and that you will be willing to continue your walk of discipleship — regardless of the path He's asking you to walk in this hour.

****

"I'm coming soon." Everyone who waits in the presence of Jesus Christ and listens to His voice hears this prophetic call. The words may differ, but the urgency remains the same.

I remember Ivan's first sermons about the Second Coming of Christ. His voice fell across the congregation with a command for attention.

"Jesus is coming back ... and this time He will come as the Righteous Judge. Are you ready for Him?"

The children stopped playing with their toys, the papers stopped rustling, and the adults sat motionless in their pews.

I listened and recalled the excitement welling up inside my own heart the first time I heard those words at a Bible study in Columbia, Maryland years before. Hearing them for the first time, I suddenly found myself a part of God's dramatic happenings here on earth as never before. Just the possibility that I might see the return of Jesus Christ stirred me with expectation and awe.

Through the 70s and into the 80s Ivan and I followed the wave of Second Coming literature pouring out of Christian publishing houses. We read the books and sang the songs heralding our Lord's return.

As Scripture promised, teacher after teacher appeared on the scene, and witnessed to one revelation from God after another. Each one described the prophetic events that would take place prior to the return of Jesus Christ.

But the years passed and Jesus didn't come back. Many prophetic events did take place, though — just as the modern day prophets foretold. We could see the changing world situation moving into line with biblical prophecy.

However, the earlier excitement that we and others experienced started to fade. It was like waiting for a promised guest who never arrives. Then one day, the phone rings and it's time. We hear him say, "I'm on my way!"

I should have heard my "spiritual telephone" ring when Charlotte taught our Adult Sunday School Class on the Second Coming. Or when a flood of End-time prophetic writings started to come my way from all over the country. But I, like so many Christians, didn't pay serious attention to the urgency rising up inside me.

Finally, Charlotte and I went head to head over the question of the Rapture and God captured my complete attention. She and I both held our stand and pointed to Scripture proofs, certain that *our* timetable for the Rapture was correct. Then we lovingly backed off by agreeing to disagree on this issue.

At home, I fell to my knees and cried out to God for answers. For weeks that turned into months, I searched for the heart of God in this matter, in the Scriptures, in discussions with other Christians, in prophetic teachings ... even in my dreams!

I boldly professed to everyone that I believed in a God who wants to speak to His people today. I needed an answer!

"Lord! Will there be a Rapture of Your Church? When? How? There are so many teachings, so many theological views. Why are we all receiving different interpretations of Your Word?"

All of my questions ignored, as though they held little significance, I could almost feel the hand of God brushing them aside.

"The Word, My daughter, is *preparation*. Prepare yourself in the ways that I will show you. Allow My Spirit to prepare you. Call others to *preparation*."

I recorded these words in my prayer diary, but it wasn't until one year later, almost to the day, that I heard from Jesus on this subject again.

For one week the Holy Spirit called me to an early morning prayer vigil. Each day I rose before dawn, prayed, and waited expectantly. At the end of the week a quiet urgency stirred in my heart. In the stillness of His presence, I waited. Then — I knew. I stood at the very threshold of a supernatural moment in time! Up from the depths of my innermost being a prophecy flowed.

> *The dawn is here. My Son is rising in majesty.*
> *The darkness is fading. Listen, My people, and pray.*
> *My Son is coming and He will fill the whole earth.*
> *He will rise up in your hearts.*
> *He will rise up in the world.*
> *Every knee will bow and every tongue confess that Jesus Christ is Lord!*
> (Matt. 25:1-13; Luke 1:78; 2 Pet. 1:19, Rev. 1:7; 1 John 2:8; Matt. 24:27; Phil. 2:10)

I sat in a moment of sacred stillness. It is time. *Jesus is on His way!*

A song filled my heart, a song calling God's people to preparation. Finally, after all these months of searching for answers — they no longer mattered. The only thing which did matter was that we were *ready*.

I searched the Word of God to find out how people had prepared for His first coming.

Mary, the mother of Jesus, found favor with God. She *heard* the voice of God's messenger. She was *obedient* (Luke 1:30,38).

Joseph *heard* the voice of God's messenger in a dream. He was *obedient* (Matt. 1:20-24).

Zechariah and Elizabeth *heard* God's prophetic word. They spoke this word in *obedience* (Luke 1:13-19, 44-45, 67-79).

John grew strong in spirit and *spoke the prophetic word* which God placed in his *hearing heart* (Luke 1:80, 3:16-18).

The shepherds were watching by night; they *heard* God's messengers and they moved in *obedience* (Luke 2:8-16).

The wise men *heard* God's voice through the prophets and moved in *obedience*. They *heard* God's message in a dream and moved in *obedience* to protect Jesus (Matt. 2:1-12).

Simeon believed the revelation of the Holy Spirit and he *prophesied* the word which God spoke to his *hearing heart* (Luke 2:25-35).

Anna fasted, prayed, prophesied, and gave thanks for the redemption of Jerusalem which God promised to her *hearing heart* (Luke 2:36-38).

All of these prepared for the first coming of Jesus had *ears to hear* the voice of God.

God spoke the *word* and created the *world*.

God spoke the *word* and sent *Jesus*.

God is *speaking the word* about our Lord's return. How many of us are listening? How many of us are ready to move in obedience to that *word*?

"The word, My daughter, is 'preparation'..."

Our spiritual Day of Preparation begins in *darkness*. The Jewish day began at evening and continued until the next evening.

The Father does things in the darkness.

Creation began in darkness (Gen. 1:2).

The Exodus of the Israelites took place in darkness (Ex. 12:42).

Jesus came as a babe in the darkness (Luke 2:8-14).

The crucifixion took place in the darkness (Matt. 27:45).

Jesus rose from the dead during the evening hours (Matt. 28:1-7).

There is no darkness *in Him*, but He moves into the darkness and makes it His covering (1 John 1:5; Ps. 139:11,12, 18:11).

Jesus enters our lives while we live in the darkness of sin and He begins to prepare us for His Coming, which will be covered in *darkness* at the day's end (Matt. 25:6).

Dawn is the first hint of light breaking through the dark night. Jesus is described as the Dawn, the Bright Morningstar (2 Pet. 1:19, Rev. 22:16). The women arrived at the tomb at early dawn (John 20:1, Luke 24:1).

Dawn is the time that we, like the women at the tomb, begin to realize that something supernatural is happening in our lives. The darkness is passing away. Some of us begin to respond to the call of Jesus, to rise up and meet the Day. Others, content to remain asleep, roll over in their comfortable spirituality and say, "I'll wake up later." But God's Word calls us to awake from our sleep (1 Thess. 5:5-6)!

Dawn gives way to *morning*. Jesus, the Bright Morningstar, rises up in our hearts. He is the Sonrise! He has been here since the hours of darkness, but now the brilliance of His light shines within us. It is time for the first light of revelation to fall upon us — the prophetic word.

The Scriptures come alive. The prophets of old and those of today speak and we listen. Jesus speaks to us in dream and vision. We know — He is on His way and His return is near.

The morning hours have always called God's people to prayer.

He sends *manna* in the morning (Ex. 16:14-15).

Great men and women of God have risen in the morning to hear His voice. We too, learn how to *listen* in the morning (Ps. 5:1-3,).

It's time to get up, to be about the Father's business just as Jesus was (John 6:38). The most productive hours are the morning hours. It is easier to work in the cool of the day and there is much work to be done in the world. Sometimes this is overwhelming and our hearts sing a song of quiet urgency and concern for the lost.

> *So many fields for planting,*
> *So many vineyards for wine,*
> *So many sheep to shepherd;*
> *Jesus, will there be time?*

We know it's morning. The entire world knows. The supernatural is moving as never before. Man's sensitivity to the spiritual forces around him is developing at a fast pace. Even the evil one summons all his forces to prepare for a coming confrontation by flooding the world with new age religions and philosophies.

What is it?

What's happening?

Everyone feels it, even those who don't understand it.

Jesus is on His way. As never before, it is imperative for us to *listen* to His words of instruction.

Why? Because *noon* is coming.

At *noon* men stumble and fall (Is. 59:10; 2 Sam. 4:5-7; 1 Kings 18:27-29; Deut. 28:28-29; Job 5:14; Jer. 6:4). Men crucified Jesus at noon (Matt. 27:45) and they will try to crucify His people.

It will be a time of intense persecution and confusion for His Body here on earth. We shall, in fact, hang on our crosses of suffering. No, these are not popular words, but they are words which I'm compelled by the Spirit to say. *Noon is coming!*

The heat of the day will beat down upon us. The light from the Son will be so bright and so intense that those who haven't learned to walk in the Light will be blinded (Acts 22:6-11).

Only those who are able to walk in the Light and *hear* the voice of God are going to know which steps to take next (Is. 30:21).

Noon is the time of false teachers and doctrine. Satan will subtly lead even the elect away (1 Tim. 4:1; Matt. 24:5, 23-24). Occult practices will become a part of

A Letter of Anticipation 167

well-meaning Christian ministries. Oppressive spirits will counterfeit the Holy Spirit, transforming Spirit-filled ministries into cult-like groups where Christians are held in bondage to leaders and teachings.

A time of darkness will cover the earth during the afternoon hours — it's the judgment of God. Jesus hung on the cross and the Father darkened the earth (Matt. 27:45). He will darken it once more. "The sun shall be turned to darkness and the moon to blood, before the Day of the Lord..." (Joel 2:30-32).

Yes, this too is going to happen during our Day of preparation (Amos 8:9).

Those who *hear and heed* the call to preparation are going to sing Psalm 91.

> ...You will not be afraid of the terror by night, or of the arrow that flies by day;
> Of the pestilence that stalks in darkness,
> Or of the destruction that lays waste at noon.
> A thousand may fall at your side,
> And ten thousand at your right hand;
> But it shall not approach you.
> You will only look with your eyes
> And see the recompense of the wicked.
> For you have made the Lord, my refuge
> Even the Most High, your dwelling place....
> Psalm 91:5-9

The day will draw to a close and to the eyes of the world, it will appear that satan has triumphed. The Body of Christ will be silenced, wrapped in a shroud of persecution and prepared for burial. Bible-believing, born-again Christians will be pronounced "dead" by the world and religious institutions alike, no longer counted as a viable force in today's society.

It is already happening! Today's prophets are shouting from the housetops! Can we deny that God's Church is being "buried" in many countries, in many of our own communities, and placed in an "underground tomb?" The Word of God is silenced in many churches, no longer given its rightful place and authority.

The persecutors of God's Church will think she is dead and boldly proclaim an end to Evangelical Christianity as we now know it.

Jesus died a physical death, once and for all. It won't be repeated. But we, the Body of Christ, are called to walk in the *spirit* as He walked to carry our cross, and to drink His cup (1 John 2:6, Mark 8:34-35). That which the enemy attempted to do to Jesus, he will again attempt to do to the Body of Christ on earth!

During the hours between the evening that Jesus was placed in the tomb and the morning of the resurrection — what happened? We confess in faith that He descended into hell to preach the Gospel to the captives (Eph. 4:9-10). He ministered to those in darkness.

We, too, while the world considers us "dead," will minister to those in darkness. The Father is going to "cover us with darkness" to preach, teach, heal, and proclaim deliverance with a power we have not known before! This "underground" Church is even now taking shape as Spirit-filled Christians are forced into hiding by world religious systems and governments.

Many of us are going to be called to abide in secret

places just as the early Christians hid in the catacombs. Although public attention won't focus on our ministry, the dynamic power of God will anoint these ministries. An "underground railway" will lead others to us for Spirit-filled ministry in the Name of Jesus.

Do not, brothers and sisters, yearn to be known, to be noticed, to be popular. Allow the Father to "cover you" in the darkness. He is doing a marvelous thing, hidden from the eyes of the world and of the evil one.

During this time, the burial shroud of persecution shall be transformed into a wedding garment of holiness! At the appointed time the Bridegroom will come (Matt. 25:6) and we will rise to meet Him!

> Arise, shine, for your light has come,
> And the glory of the Lord has risen upon you.
> For behold, darkness will cover the earth,
> And deep darkness the peoples,
> But the Lord will rise upon you
> And His glory will appear upon you.
> And nations will come to your light
> And kings to the brightness of your rising.
>
> Isaiah 60:1-3

One word will make the difference and that word is *preparation*. You've heard it from the Holy Spirit just as I have. It made the difference for Jesus and it is going to make the difference for us.

Jesus had *ears to hear* the Father each hour of the day. He walked in complete *obedience*. He allowed the Father to "set apart" (to sanctify, to make holy) His life from the sinful world He lived in. Tempted at every turn, He walked in *holiness* before the Father.

170 *A Church Without Walls*

Give thanks to the Father for the disciplines of your faith, for the trials, for the times of silent endurance, for the race set before you.

He's preparing you.

He's preparing me.

He's breaking down the walls that divide us, building a Church without walls. All that we might stand in readiness, together, as the Bride of Christ, to meet the Bridegroom in the sky.

Alleluia, my friend, will you listen to me?
Are you ready for Jesus, His glory to see?
Jesus is coming, He's coming again,
Are you ready for Jesus? Are you ready, my friend?

Chapter Nine

A Letter of Instruction to a Church Without Walls

Dear Brothers and Sisters in Christ:

We're rejoicing with you in this hour. Your listening heart and your walk of obedience have led you to a wide place of ministry.

Although your church buildings surround you, they no longer imprison you. The multitudes join you, but they do not impress you. Religious labels often confront you, but they do not intimidate you.

The walls of religiousity are insignificant in comparison with the Church you see rising in the midst of God's people. *It's a house without walls, built of living stones, and you abide within it.*

Your eyes now envision a work much greater than denominational kingdoms and evangelical empires. You see the Father's House — *without the walls of division or limitations.*

Its boundaries stretch from the vineyards of love to the valleys of healing, across the waters of faith and into the battlefields of yesterday. It gives birth to new ministries and nurtures the multitudes with a heart of love.

Wherever open ears and obedient hearts are found, you find a room in the Father's House. There, among the brethren, your quest for *understanding* is understood and encouraged.

Jesus reminds you, "Be not afraid of the work I am doing in this hour." Like the walls of Jericho, *the walls of fear within you have come down.*

Above all, you're broken. The hardness of your heart is gone. The Father smiles at the new spirit within you. It's teachable ... gentle ... willing.

Our hearts are encouraged and lifted up because we hear that you are fellowshiping together, ministering to one another in the Name of Jesus, and earnestly seeking His Divine will (Matt. 9:37-38).

As you grow in spirit and in number, it is essential to once again emphasize the basic disciplines of a "listening heart" so you'll not be led astray by the evil one. Thus, we write to you, not as children who need to learn, but to those who have already learned and stand ready to teach (2 Tim. 3:14-17, Is. 50:4-5).

Spend time with your Lord.

Be still in His presence. Be silent.

Let all that resounds through your heart and mind learn to be silent before Him.

Learn to listen to the silence, for in it you will soon recognize a language of love which transcends all human perception of words and thoughts. It's the

Shepherd of Love Himself, reaching out and calling you unto Himself (John 16:12-15, Rev. 3:22, Jer. 33:3, John 10:4).

Speak with Him often, but speak tender words of love and adoration. Put aside the selfish attitude which only has time to receive from God. Give your love with a thankful heart. He loves you more than any man. He waits for your response as the Bridegroom waits for His Bride.

Never forget the necessity for continual "spiritual housecleaning." Submit to the Lordship of Jesus. Confess your sins, involvement in unholy activities and the works of darkness.

Spirits of darkness are eagerly waiting to speak words of deception to those of us who (knowingly and unknowingly) participate in their evil schemes. Teach, encourage, and exhort those who are new in the faith to renounce the works of darkness and ask for the Blood of Jesus to cleanse them from all sin (James 5:13-16, Gal. 5:19-21, Eph. 5:7-14, 1 John 1:9, Deut. 18:9-14).

Be bold as you pray for one another and in the laying on of hands. Pray for spiritual eyes and ears to be opened in the Name of Jesus. Pray for the gifts of discernment, revelation, and, above all, wisdom.

Remember, however, that before this prayer is offered for anyone, this individual must be yielded to the Lord Jesus Christ, openly and lovingly professing Him as Savior and Lord (Matt. 10:32).

Do not shirk the responsibility before you — to inquire with love, "Do you know Jesus Christ as Savior and Lord?"

Shake off the shackles of condemnation which have bound you to the *walls of tradition*. Christ has set you free!

Now go in His Name and open the prison doors! Others are waiting to share in your freedom from eternal punishment (2 Tim. 4:1-5, Gal. 5:1).

It is impossible to say these things often enough, for it's only by the Holy Spirit, who dwells within us when we receive Jesus as Savior and Lord, that we *hear and understand* the will of our Heavenly Father (1 John 4:15).

Lay hands upon one another and pray expectantly for Jesus to baptize with His Holy Spirit, for the release of spiritual gifts, and for anointing in ministry. Stir up the gifts that are within you. Take each other by the hand and kneel before the Throne of Grace and Love. Pray and praise until the angels in heaven are rejoicing with you — come forth with a bold confidence you've not known before! (2 Tim. 1:6-7, Mark 1:8, Heb. 4:16, Luke 11:13)

Although we learn to be silent before Him, it is important to remind you again — it's quite impossible to *learn* to manifest the prophetic gifts (or any gift from God). These are gifts, initiated and given by the Holy Spirit Himself. We make ourselves available to receive them with a willing heart, never seeking the gift, always seeking He who gives.

We learn to be silent. We learn to wait. We learn to open our mouths in obedience, but it is always the Holy Spirit who must fill them (1 Cor. 12:11, 2 Pet. 1:19-21, Heb. 2:3-4).

Beware of spirits seeking to counterfeit God's gifts

with "techniques" and "laws" for receiving the manifestations of the Holy Spirit. Always remember — it's impossible to "learn" a gift (1 John 4:1-6).

Make time to listen in silence together, with one heart. For in this time, the anointing of God will bind you together in Him. It's a relationship of oneness with each other and with the Father which will see you through the days ahead. Jesus has already asked the Father to grant this gift to you — receive it with thanksgiving (John 17:20-23).

Draw near together in praise and worship, moving into a time of silence before the King of Kings and Lord of Lords. At the close of the silence, speak gently to one another about your *understanding* of God's Word in your heart.

Confirm one another, build one another up, and pray for one another. As you do, His Holy Spirit will bind you together with cords of compassion and love. Everyone cries for unity, yet so few are willing to allow the Spirit of God to manifest the unity of *His Spirit* among them (Rom. 8:26-27, Col. 3:12-17, 1 Cor. 2:1-13).

Ivan and I are praying for this unity in Spirit among you, for without it you will be a "mixed multitude" destined to wander in a spiritual wilderness. It's imperative for you to become one with those with whom you are in fellowship.

The sin of selfish pride has ruled in the Body of Christ for too long, each insisting upon his own way, building insurmountable walls.

Wherever the Holy Spirit calls you together — in the fields, on the mountains, in livingrooms, in the sanctuaries, or in fellowship halls —

Worship together!
Listen together!
Walk together!
Be the Body of Christ! (1 Cor. 12:12)

Beware of seducing spirits attempting to counterfeit the unity of the Holy Spirit by entwining you with cords of bondage to a ministry or leader. Such spirits will exercise control by convincing you that everyone should speak the same words, pray the same prayers, and minister according to prescribed formulas. *Uniformity is a counterfeit for unity.*

Godly leaders will not hand you easy answers. They'll point you to Jesus Christ and help you to struggle with issues of faith. They will not call for loyalty and total submission *to a ministry*. Instead, they'll ask you to submit to Jesus Christ and to serve Him *through a ministry*. Be watchful of subtle twisting spirits.

The Spirit of God always *builds* upon the foundation He has already laid in your life. He doesn't tear it down. He doesn't send you through the graveyards of your past and ask you to dig up past sin, covered by His Blood and forgiven in His Name. Do not be surprised, however, if you encounter deceiving spirits which entice you to "make certain every sin is covered by the prayers of *our ministry*."

Flee from such works! Hold fast to that which is good! Hold fast to that which is right and according to the Word of God! Hold fast to the steadfast love of God in your life!

Always treat those things the Lord says among you with respect, awe, and reverence. As He inscribes His

Word on your heart, record this word for your mind to ponder and meditate on in the days ahead.

Encourage one another to keep a prayer diary — a prayer journal. Much of God's Word to us is not understood with wisdom until the passing of time. This takes days, months, and sometimes even years. Those who have walked before us have recorded His Word ... shall we do any less?

Martin Luther encouraged the early Church of the Reformation to give honor to the Holy Spirit and to write down prophetic revelation. How much have we lost through the generations by not giving such honor to God? (Matt. 24:35, Rev. 1:11)

He sends His Word (written and prophetic) forth to accomplish that for which it is intended. Therefore, it is sent for a specific purpose and very often for a specific moment in time.

He watches over His Word to perform it! If He watches over it, shall we do any less? Do not speak such words with careless thought. Do not toss them about and scatter them in the wind like wild seed. *Sow the seed with prayerful thought and wisdom — do not throw the seed!*

Test all prophetic revelations. Write them down and submit them to the leader or leaders among you for discernment and prayer. This is especially important for those of you who are young in listening prayer!

Submit your revelations for judgment according to (1) The written Word of God (2) The spirit in which it is given (3) The confirmation of two or more witnesses (4) The fulfillment. Hold fast to that which is good! (1 John 4:1, 1 Thess. 5:19-22, 1 Cor. 14:13-33)

If there is a questionable revelation among you, please don't allow it to become a foothold for dissension. Quietly lay it aside and wait. If it's of God, it will stand. If not, it will pass away.

We're still human. Our listening heart won't be perfect until we meet Him face to face.

Let everyone submitting a word do so with a servant's heart, treating each other with respect in the Lord, as co-workers in the Kingdom of God. Women, so richly gifted with a sensitive listening ear, always be ready to allow the Spirit to bring balance to your gifts through the voices of the men in authority over you.

Men, so abundantly blessed with steadfastness, the Lord will hold you responsible for priestly obedience and service. Respect the burning word in your heart, for it is the fire of God. Be not afraid to open your mouths and proclaim the words aflame within you. One word aflame resounds through the Kingdom and lights more hearts for Jesus than dozens of little sparks.

Submit your words to one another in the Lord and together, as godly men, you will form an umbrella of priestly protection over your families and fellowship. Do not take your obedience in the prophetic ministry lightly! (Phil. 2:1-11, 1 Thess. 5:12-32, Heb. 13:17)

Women, don't be afraid to speak, to share, to question — knowing that it is not *the words you say, but the spirit in which you say them* which makes the difference. Speak softly and in love. Never use your words (or emotions) to hold authority over any man. Rather, submit your words as an offering of love (1 Pet. 3:1-6).

Men, listen to these offerings. Weigh them. Test them. Take up your responsibility of authority without fear, for it is *Christ in you* who leads the way. In many areas of your lives you walk tall and strong. Now, rise up in the Name of Jesus. It was to the disciples, the men, that Jesus first called, "Follow Me!" (Mark 1:17, 2:14).

In the Scriptures we see women learning while sitting at the feet of Jesus. Many of those among you have spent many hours at His feet. The men, however, learned by walking beside Him, by participating in ministry, one step at a time. They were equipped and taught as they followed. He spoke with them *on the way!* (Luke 10:38-42, Mark 8:27)

Everyone, never forget that the prophetic word (that which we hear with a listening heart) grows from the seed of the *written Word*. Nothing of God comes to us apart from His written Word!

The seed is planted as we hear, read, study, and pray His written Word. It is watered as we pray and praise, beseeching the Father to know and understand His heart. The words we hear, the visions we see, the dreams we dream — they're all like buds in springtime. We see the future promise, but we don't understand it completely and we shall not until the day of its fulfillment.

On that day the prophetic word will burst into full bloom and we will know without a doubt that *God has spoken!* The final confirmation of prophecy is and always will be its fulfillment.

On each of these thoughts there is so much already written — in the Word of God, in many books, and on your own hearts. Our call from the Spirit today is to "stir up" that which you've already received in Him and *to encourage you to teach others.*

To this end, we pray that you abide in His Word, continue in prayer, and walk in obedience to the prophetic word now coming forth in your fellowships. We pray that your spiritual eyes and ears be healed and opened anew to the Word of Obedience coming forth in this hour, that the gifts of ministry abound among you, and that you lead others to Jesus Christ and produce much fruit in the Kingdom of God (Eph. 1, Phil. 1:6, Matt. 28:18-20).

Open the doors of your home, your fellowship, and your church to those who are weary. The Father's House has no walls within it — He has only your lives to form *circles of love and ministry* for a broken world and, in many cases, a broken Church.

The temples of "religious form" are crumbling all around us like sand castles. The wounded are searching for a place of refuge. Speak boldly in the Name of Jesus to the *walls of fear* in their hearts and say, "Be not afraid."

Love in the Name of Our Lord Jesus,
The Koberleins

Then up from the valley
  To the mountain we'll climb,
To the vineyards of love
  And the fruit of the vine,
One with another our lives there entwined,
  Together we'll pray and drink of new wine.

Chapter Ten

The final chaper belongs to you. It will be written on the parchment of your life by the Holy Spirit as the Father uses you, a living stone, to build *His Church Without Walls.*

LOVE YE ONE ANOTHER

Where are you going?
    What do you see?
Uncaring strangers
    That were once a family
They don't understand
    God's forgiving plan.

People next to people
    Standing row to row
Knowing not each other
    Crowded yet so alone
Wounded, weak and weary
    They don't understand
God's plan of salvation
    Given unto man.

Love and understanding
    They provide the key
To unlock man's heart and feeling
    So he's not alone, you see
Love ye one another
    Live out God's command
Reach out for your brothers
    In God's family of man.

                              JG

And I lifted my eyes and saw, and behold, a man with a measuring line in his hand! Then I said, "Where are you going?"

And he said to me, "To measure Jerusalem to see what is its breadth and what is its length."

And behold, the angel who talked with me came forward, and another angel came forward to meet him, and said to him, "Run, say to that young man, *'Jerusalem shall be inhabited as villages without walls,* because of the multitudes of men and cattle in it.' "

"For I will be to her a wall of fire round about, "says the Lord," and I will be the glory within her."

Zechariah 2:1-5

The Koberleins may be contacted at:

The Open Door Ministry
P.O. Box 9052
Bethlehem, PA 18018